Unfinished Business
A Banker Looks at the Economy

ALSO BY THE AUTHOR

Paul M. Mazur

Unfinished Business
A Banker Looks at the Economy

Nash Publishing, Los Angeles

Library of Congress Catalog Card Number: 73-83521
International Standard Book Number: 0-8402-1321-2

Published simultaneously in the United States and Canada
by Nash Publishing Corporation, 9255 Sunset Boulevard,
Los Angeles, California 90069.

Printed in the United States of America.

First Printing.

To my wife, with love

Contents

Preface

The adverse reaction that manifested itself in the U.S. economy starting in 1969 was not considered by most economists or economic observers as particularly severe. In fact, many applied to it the label of "mini-recession." But a mini-recession or even a stagnation in the commerce and industry of a nation whose dimensions are those of the United States can have serious and far-reaching repercussions. If the expected secular growth of an annual gross national product of over 1 trillion dollars amounts to 4 percent, the replacement of that figure, not with a decline, but a zero amount, means a yearly practical loss of 40 billions of dollars. Generally, the economy in all of its phases has become accustomed to the face and voice of expansion. Its expenses, wages, profits, and taxes are geared to the *expected* growth of the country's income. When this growth does not occur for a year, then about 40 billion dollars gross and the resultant component parts disappear into never-never land. And if a mild mini-recession, or even stagnation, extends over a period of three years, the cumulative total in terms of GNP reaches the colossal figure of 120 billions of dollars. Government deficits or serious retrenchment in the public sector, or both, may be one result. And the private segment will show adverse or even unhealthy signs in the well-being of the nation's economy.

The recession which started in 1969 manifested obstinate resistance in emerging from its doldrums. Then, in spite of *emergence* from rather than entry into active war, the economy began to heat up and assume some characteristics of an economic boom.

This euphoric condition obtained even with the existence of unbalanced budgets, badly imbalanced international payments, and periodic monetary crises and devaluations of the dollar. The heady experience of rising economic trends held despotic sway for a relatively short time. By early 1973, in spite of favorable reports on business, employment, real wages, and profits, there began to appear questions and doubts about how long these favorable conditions would continue. Prognostications for the future became divided between those who maintained their full optimism and the ones who saw threatening clouds and even foul economic weather ahead.

Prices in security markets broke badly. Drastic shortages appeared, not only in meat and fuel, but in wool, lumber, and other materials as well. Excess productive capacities appeared to fade into a conviction of inadequate facilities; and surplus labor was said to be disappearing to be replaced by substantial deficits in many areas.

Inflation, it was claimed, was again upon a trend of rapid escalation. And with this observation and prophecy, there came the companion conclusion that rising prices would not be accepted by the country's consumers but be vetoed daily in the market baskets that serve as their true and continuous ballot boxes.

Which school of economic thinking will prove to be valid perhaps will be written in the tomorrows. All that one seems able to hold as a certain conviction is that there is *no* unanimity in the "art" of economics, and that the devices presently used seem to be lacking seriously not only in their accuracy, but even their adequacy as well.

And in spite of all one's misgivings, there must exist the conviction that the act and fact of economics represent such a *very, very* important phase, even requirement, for the successful attainment of man's material well-being.

There is a higher order of existence where all quantitative explanations fail, where thought must turn from the measurable to the qualitative, and from what merely is to what ought to be.

From The Power of Silence, *1895*
HORATIO W. DRESSER

PART I:
SOME DIVERGENT POINTS OF VIEW

1.
In the Beginning

Economics is not an exact science nor can it be labeled an art. It is a sprawling, flexible, amorphous body of facts and varying theories and interpretations. But the prosperity, stability, and material well-being of societies are founded upon economic heritage, whether accidental or planned.

As an observer of economic events over five decades, I have concluded that many of the present and past approaches to our economic problems miss the mark. Moreover, the faults are not only those of commission but of omission. We have taken many wrong steps and have failed to take many right ones.

My chief concern has been with the pragmatics of economics in business as I saw it actually at work in the operation of a score or more corporate institutions. Perhaps my contacts, being chiefly with business, have given me a viewpoint toward the economy different from that of men who have spent their working lives primarily in academia.

I seriously question the validity of a quantitative basis as the foundation of our economic reasoning, conclusions, and policies. And I would propose building our major economic concepts upon the humanistic, social, and natural qualitative factors created by the people in a society. Finally, I would like to see the present form and ritual in economics replaced by a concern for the material relationships of human beings.

In the theory and practice of economic control of our society, there seems to be a hiatus between the theory of practice and the practice of theory. Whether the approach is monetary or fiscal, economic control seems increasingly to rely upon mathematics, or "econometrics," or upon some principle built on a theoretical base and developed through induction or deduction. And, often, national policies—particularly those created by central governmental agencies—have had their genesis in these relatively abstract mathe-matical premises that some able luminaries of the "word" have developed and promoted. This approach has frequently devalued and neglected the more human and pragmatic side of economics.

I believe that our economy is influenced, or even governed, more by *qualitative* than by *quantitative* factors. The qualitative factors within our economy are primarily people, their characteristics, their way of life, their environment, inventiveness, productivity, education, habits, and psychological attitudes. How people live and work, how they multiply their numbers, increase their productivity, express their creativity, fulfill their desires, and raise their standards of living are among the qualitative aspects of any economy.

Quantitative factors, either in an economy or in economics, are basically mathematical. Among these I would include the supply of money and credit, the rates of interest, the manipulation of bank reserves, the tax and fiscal policies of the governments (including deficits, surpluses, credits and gifts to other nations), the plans and acts of investment in capital assets, the statistical result of people's spending or saving programs—all of which, in turn, are influenced qualitatively.

Quantitative economics as a governing ideology now seems almost all-pervading, in concept and procedure. Its influence is growing with the increasing sophistication of our electronic computing devices. Although there appears to be a greater awareness of the importance of the qualitative factors in our society, they are still relegated to a junior status among the causal ingredients of our economy. Nevertheless, it is the qualitative characteristics that determine our living patterns and the state of our economy. The needs and acts of the human beings in our society may have quantitative economic consequences, but their genesis is qualitative.

Not too long ago I attended a luncheon in midtown Manhattan at which the main speaker was the chief executive of an important air-transport corporation. He was a leader in commercial aviation and a great advocate of its value. He talked chiefly about the difficulties that aviation faces.

He said that from the brains of men there have come new and dramatic designs that will increase both the capacity and speed of commercial planes, and that these would require substantial capital for construction, operation, and maintenance. On the other hand, they would add significantly to the demand for labor and supplies.

Beyond the costs that relate to the plane itself there are many others, he said, that will also escalate. The supervision of four hundred passengers enplaning onto and deplaning from a single commercial airliner will demand new mechanics of handling; new terminals built on recently acquired and more expensive land; and new roads or other means of transportation to and from airports. When air travel has increased over the next decade by another 50 percent, what will the situation be regarding the movement of passengers to and from the terminals? Will billions of dollars of new investment be required for new and very expensive road systems? And, if so, how will the necessary rights-of-way through high-cost real estate districts be financed, or even obtained? Or will new railroad systems or newly created monorail routes be established from cities' central points to the airports? And how will these be financed and what effect will they have on taxes, if publicly owned, or on air-transportation rates, if privately financed?

While the probable consequences are beyond the imagination of most of us, some of them are visible, at least in vague outlines. Shall we have a satellite system of helicopters and short takeoff and landing planes that will start from areas in or near the cities, perhaps from lakes or rivers or bays where land has been man-made for the purpose? Will the present inadequate railway terminals and tracks and rolling stock be required to carry the load of more millions of plane travelers? Or will the present problems affect, even relocate, the future trade centers of nations because the present major metropolises and centers of trade have become choked by their own internal traffic and transportation paralysis?

The executive's talk was impressive mainly because he spoke about his problems and some of those of the society that he and his industry must live in, in practical, down-to-earth terms. He touched on some of the causes, consequences, and expectations of the sociological—and political —environmental difficulties that wrap themselves around his industry like the snakes that strangled Laocoön; but he described the situation in qualitative language, not in orthodox quantitative terms. He never referred to a single monetary fact or factor, to the price of gold, or to the balance of trade or payments.

The basic or causal factors that impose their force upon the economy will be qualitatively human, scientific, psychological, biological, political, and sociological. Huge fiscal, monetary, and quantitative consequences will flow from either the successful solution of the problems or their catastrophic neglect. But to emphasize the quantitative aspects to the neglect of the qualitative is to fail, indeed, to see the trees for the forest.

Among the many economic panaceas extant, there appears to be only one that has won general acceptance. That is, constant growth. But there is no consensus as to how continuous growth can best be assured.

I believe the major emphasis should be on qualitative, not quantitative factors; not on the mathematical or econometric but the human and sociological. And when stimuli ail or die, the economy will suffer from their loss or weakness unless their health is restored or new stimuli created to take their place.

As I contemplate the parade of experiences, people, and conclusions that have passed in my view, I like to believe that some of the lessons that time has distilled for me may be of general interest. I review the past and soliloquize about what the future may hold.

The thrust of the thesis of this volume is primarily economic, not political or social. I have tried to present whatever I have written in nontechnical language. I hope the effort has not been in vain. This volume has been written laboriously in longhand over many months starting early in 1970. Since then, I have read printed references to ideas similar or ever.

identical to several of my own. Rather than regret this coincidence, I welcome it, since it confirms their validity—at least to a degree.

The economy, as an active, integral part of life in the United States, is truly an entire pattern made up of inter-related and correlated threads. Each part should be subject to review and interpretation only as a component of the whole. But the total economy, with all its complexities, must always be viewed as a complete unit.

2.
A Rebel in the Ranks: Qualitative vs. Quantitative

I would guess that one hundred times the effort and money expended on the study of qualitative factors are spent on debates that take place all over the Western world among the thousands who review, measure, remeasure, and hope to modify, even in a minuscule way, the problems of the gold standard. They seek possible substitutes for it—a new medium of international currency to expedite world trade and relieve the terrifying crises that constantly recur.

If a high-ranking treasury official offhandedly says he believes all monetary choices—including gold prices—should be left open, there is panic in the markets and a rush by speculators to buy more gold. If he says nothing, the interpretation can be about the same: because he did *not* say gold would not go up in price, and say it with emphasis and sincerity, he really meant that the price could and probably *would* go up.

Monetary meetings seem to be devoted almost exclusively to the search for some palliative for financial problems and dangers—not to their causes. To many, gold is still a very important criterion of a nation's solvency, but it is difficult, if not impossible, to trace the interaction of gold with prices and monetary stability. For decades, from the early thirties until recently, gold has played no *direct* part in the exchange of goods and services. It is equally difficult to trace the maze of routes by which the gold supplies in Fort Knox, the subtreasury, the Federal Reserve vaults, and the central banks influence the daily trading activity of millions of corporations and billions of people. Practically all barter of goods for goods for services, services for services, and services for goods is accomplished without invoking the values assumed to reside in gold itself and without awareness of gold as a reserve.

It must be obvious that unless the amount of gold were enormously—truly enormously—increased, its supply would be *inadequate* for the transaction requirements, not only of tomorrow, but of today.

The known gold reserves of governments and central banks are now valued at about $50 billion—mostly in the form of inert bullion bars stored away in expensively and well-guarded vaults. If this golden treasure truly served as a base for the currencies, transactions, and trade of the world, there would exist the extraordinary phenomenon represented by a lever calibrated in gold moving and balancing the total weight of trade of the world business dealings. Although not actually measurable, they are reasonably estimated at nearly three trillion dollars annually, or one dollar of gold for every sixty dollars of world transactions. This calculation assumes, of course, that all other claims once or now "payable" in gold have lost their rights and can be liquidated only by the payment in other paper claims—just as is already true in the case of United States currency.

If any device or decision resulted in a substantial increase in the annual production of gold, that growth would come primarily from the contribution by the Russian and the South African mines. The USSR and South Africa would be almost the sole beneficiaries of the greater supply of the precious yellow metal dug from the bowels of the earth—but only from the earth in two localities.

If gold supplies were increased under the stimulus of a higher declared price that usually is made by edict, not by free markets, then that decision would probably have to be made chiefly by the United States, because its policy of purchasing all gold offerings at thirty-five dollars an ounce was the main support under the price of gold over the past four decades until 1971. And an increase in the gold price by edict, again chiefly through the cooperation and power of the United States, would raise the floor of gold and depreciate the value of the paper money that must be offered in exchange. Then those nations that had shown their faith in the United States and kept their reserves intact, and had not demanded gold for large dollar balances, would be rewarded for their cooperation by being forced to take huge losses. By the same token, nations that had taken much from the largess of the United States and had given little or no cooperation would be rewarded by a special premium in increased prices for the gold they drew from this country by converting all or most of their dollar claims into actual ownership of the yellow specie.

However, even if the advocacy of the fiction of an adequate increase in gold production were feasible, and even if a successful campaign actually created a rise in the official price of gold, how important and how permanent would the result prove to be? *Unless the trade and transactions among nations came into balance and remained so, after a short time the rivulet of gold would again run downhill away from the lands of surplus imports to those of excess exports.*

In other words, gold—unless it can be manufactured by

practically everybody in unlimited amounts with the magic of alchemists—will not remain as a stable deposit in the same vaults of the world's banks. It will travel, eventually, in accordance with the demands of trade and the balance of payments; or it will remain securely domiciled in its established homes so long as the nations' foreign accounts remain in equilibrium.

It is the reality of the *international transaction balance* that is the important part of the international economic equation; for gold is useful as a reserve only when it is not eroded by a payment's imbalance. Into the jaws of demand, made by national balances of payments, disappear goods exported and imported, services bought and sold, interest and dividend payments made and received, travelers' expenditures created abroad, capital investments over long periods or for short-time loans, expenditures required for armed forces stationed abroad in excess of the monies spent domestically for that purpose, and gifts and loans for foreign aid in excess of the portion of these funds expended within the limits of the donors' own countries.

The list is long and not always stable. It reacts in identification and amount to *needs*, to the political *temper* of the grantor, to the reciprocal *attitudes* and acts of the beneficiaries from mutual friendliness to unilateral antagonism—in short, to qualitative factors and influences. *Neither the price of gold nor the abracadabra of monetary meetings held to discuss the problems and discover new devices have altered this truth.*

As though in recognition of this, President Nixon, on August 15, 1971, as part of a drastic and comprehensive economic plan, ended the convertibility of the dollar into gold and cut it free from a fixed rate of exchange. The currency of the United States was thereby allowed to float freely in world markets. Other nations followed suit quickly;

and two weeks later Japan severed the yen from its moorings of a fixed rate. By September 1, 1971, the United States dollar was floated in terms of foreign exchange. A termination of the attempts to retain the impossible conversion of dollars into gold out of a hopelessly inadequate supply—the anachronistic tie of currency to its theoretical stated gold equivalent—seemed finally to have been severed, belatedly, but at long last.

Increasingly, the plan of adopting freely floating exchange rates among international currencies had been receiving favorable attention. After all, beef, corn, wheat, clothing, appliances, and carrots do not have fixed prices but prices that float directly within their own circumference and indirectly within the general level of all prices. Why should exchange rates not be subject to the same kind of influences?

On May 10, 1971, the German mark was separated from a fixed exchange rate and allowed to float in relation to the prices of other currencies. It quickly sold at a premium over the United States dollar; or, obversely, the dollar sold at a discount in terms of the price of the mark. How long this freely floating exchange rate will last is indeterminate. It may be stabilized by dictum, at least for a while. Or a stability may be achieved, de facto, by the establishment and maintenance of an equilibrium between exports and imports for both visible and invisible items.

The adoption of freely floating exchange would reflect the actual facts of the barter relationship among nations and allow for natural adjustments to correct the disequilibriums of trade, capital, and services that skew the balance of payments. Nations with import surpluses would experience discounts on their exchange rates in the international markets. Excesses of exports would create premiums in prices for the products of those nations with surpluses of sales or services in world markets.

A number of academicians hold firmly to the belief that it is the fluctuation in the flow of money that controls the price level and the state of the economy. Within the cult there are many able students. They chart the flow of money into the economy and indicate, or at least imply, its effect. Although squares and lines and arrows are integral parts of organization and flow charts, placing them neatly on paper does not make them either conclusive or logical, or even understandable.

How does a flow of 4 percent of increased currency or money into the veins and arteries of the economy actually affect wages, savings, the desire to purchase, and the acts of buying? What solid historical evidence is there of the actual relationship between the amount of currency or money and a country's material well-being? And what factual and valid statistical and historical support is there for the theory that the quantity of money has ever influenced the state of commerce and industry? Why has it been necessary for these advocates to change the content of their monetary formulas or potions over the years? What role is played, not by the amount of money or currency in the economy, but by the *velocity* with which these media of exchange or purchasing power carom from the pocket of one individual or corporate buyer to a seller, and from him to another buyer, and so on through the turnover of many transactions?

Unhappily, one finds himself again in intellectual quick-sand or an economic bog. One can neither prove incontrovertibly that the monetary thesis is patently invalid, nor validate its truth.

But when a pig or a coat is sold and bought for so many pieces of money or chits that are only promises to pay, those involved in the transaction will be hard put to find out how they, as buyers or sellers, are affected by the drip, drip, drip of currency into the circulatory system of the economy.

The unquestioned leader of the monetary school of economics is Milton Friedman, Paul Snowden Russell Distinguished Service Professor in the Department of Economics at the University of Chicago. Over the years, he has presented many original, persuasive, brilliant, and valid theses relating to our political-economic society. Although I regret that I am unable to agree with Professor Friedman's specific theory that money is the controlling factor in the trends of our economy, I sincerely believe him to be one of the outstanding and truly original thinkers and advocates among all our economists.

Another method of economic control that formerly had many adherents and exerted great force was the manipulation of interest rates. This piece of economic legerdemain has apparently lost much of its magic. It still has its advocates, however, and it is still of substantial importance in shifting liquid international funds to the markets that pay the highest prices.

But the adherents who pay obeisance to interest rates as the means of modifying and controlling economic trends have lost many of their followers. Effective nominal interest rates that exist as residual costs in the operation of business never total more than one-half the gross cost of the interest charges. In the past, if a bond or a loan carried a rate of 4 percent, the actual effect upon the earnings after taxes was about 50 percent (about one-half of the 4 percent), or 2 percent. If the interest rate on bonds or any other kind of loans increases to 9 percent, then the effective rate that influences profits after taxes will again be one-half, or 4½ percent. The difference between a low cost of 2 percent and a high rate of 4½ percent is substantial; but it is after all only 2½ percent after taxes. That margin, dramatic as it appears, is not likely to act as a serious deterrent to investments for which long-term capital is usually raised through loans. And the "real" interest charge is further reduced as a result of inflation's erosion of the dollar's value.

Under these circumstances, interest rates probably must rise almost astronomically before they, *by their own pressure,* deter the expansion of capital investment by business corporations. Moreover, it is entirely likely that business planners accept increased interest rates—like increased taxes—as a rise in the price of one or more of the ingredients in the total-cost formula and, therefore, part of the package that must be paid for by the buyers. To the extent that increased prices affect the economy, rising interest rates, which are usually components of cost, will probably have their influence upon the volume of business.

When interest charges are substantial portions of cost, and the debt assumed by the buyer runs for protracted periods of time, the effect of rising interest rates as a deterrent can be far greater. Consumer installment purchases, however, would probably not be too adversely affected by somewhat higher interest costs—*if the time over which the required liquidation of the debt extends could be augmented.* But for single housing units, procured primarily on long-term mortgages extending for twenty years or longer, it is difficult to lengthen the period still further. For the buyers of such products, the force of rising cost of borrowing could have a direct, undiluted, and powerful impact—probably even greater than the more-talked-about rise in the cost of the building lot, the materials, and the on-site labor, significant as all of these actually are.

The availability of capital and the influence of the monetary mechanism have infinitely more far-reaching effects than interest and tax rates. The terms "shortage," "squeeze," and "crunch" have, at various times, been applied to the scarcity of the flow of capital and to credit from the banks to industry and commerce. The year 1966 represented a high-water mark for the low-water level of available credit. That was the year of the "great crunch."

But even then, selected clients could obtain large sums for the productive needs of their business as well as for what, in a sense, was a nonproductive use—to finance tenders for the shares of other companies in the epidemic of "take-overs" that began its crescendo about the year of the "great credit crunch."

A shortage of capital or credit is always a restraint on business activity. It is even possible to imagine a shortage or crunch so serious as to hamper the flow of capital and credit necessary to the economy. For modern economies live on and by credit; and much of the capitalization that comes from the savings of thousands of investors depends on the credit status of the borrowers. Nor is all the credit of capital offered by the lenders actually hard cold cash from the accumulation of savings. For some of it, the creditor calls on credit for himself, which he converts into capital for the borrower.

Capital and credit are like Siamese twins. They seem different; but they act as though they were inseparable parts of the same organic system.

It is said that capital is the creation of the savings of men and of corporate units. Perhaps it is. But often what is capital today grew out of the use of credit that was built, not on granite, but on sand, sometimes quicksand, and often on hope, faith, courage, nerve, and perhaps hazardous risks. If the gambles paid off, the gambler became an important capitalist, even an economic statesman.

Two groups of ardent advocates are busily engaged in surveying and constructing alternate routes for our economy.

The more numerous group is plotting its course carefully and methodically by using all the modern mathematical devices available: micrometers, microscopes, and electronic computers. I ally myself with a much smaller—though equally dedicated—group that plots its route, not by quantitative means, but by qualitative analyses of our society. Our tools are biological, anthropological, sociological, and psychological. We are concerned mainly with the people who make the economy; with how they activate it, and how they, in turn, are influenced by it.

3.
Credit:
The Economic Mystique

Without a *supply* of credit—an adequate supply—the modern system of economics will reduce its speed or grind slowly to a complete halt. On the other hand, credit availability, even in large quantities, does not guarantee that trade will be highly active or prosperity assured. Often, credit is cheapest and most plentiful when the economy is substantially depressed. The availability of funds at such a time will not assure their acceptance or use.

Like currency or money, credit acts *primarily* as a lubricant in our complex economic mechanisms. Like a lubricant, it helps the machinery of trade to run more smoothly and with less friction. Although credit may on occasion be a stimulant to business, it rarely, *by itself,* supplies the whole economy with enough generative stimuli. Even though its absence or shortage may contract the tempo of business, its availability is not likely to reverse a downward to a rising trend.

The economy can be adversely affected more by a lack of credit than by a stringency in currency, even though, as a device, the exchange of goods for currency is highly preferable to the simple, naked barter of things and services in kind. However, the economy can figuratively drown in a flood of credit. Like the lone castaway on a desert island who has no use for the treasure of gold or jewels he may find there, an excess of money and credit in an economically discouraged, depressed society can be a sterile contribution, not creating any equivalent desire or demand.

Like the monetary supply, credit is an essential ingredient of modern economic societies. But unlike money, the sources of credit, its location, its actual courses of travel after creation and acceptance, and its final destination are not subject to detailed delineation and are not so clearly defined.

As far as I know, there is no published volume that treats the subject of credit clearly, definitively, and persuasively. Its dimensions are lost in a fog. Its sources and its disposition are not always traceable, and often appear to be somewhat vague and variable. Although the flow of currency also influences the economy in mysterious ways, credit is the true enigma of our business complex.

While the claim is made, probably with a good deal of validity, that credit reacts to the old, well-established law of supply and demand, the elements that contribute to its availability and use are by no means apparent.

Most of us probably think of credit as flowing primarily from the conventional banking and savings system of the nation. Although huge sums do emanate from the people and from banks, there are other sources that are more important in the current operations of our economy. Many of these, not specifically identified with banks, furnish funds in huge amounts for the needs and demands of the economy.

The most notable and largest of these sources are those

that create a huge volume of trade by the devices of accounts receivable and accounts payable. With the creation of these bookkeeping transactions, corporate units offer credit for varying periods to their customers; and buyers are willing to assume the obligations to make repayment of principal and interest at the maturity dates prescribed. Granting loans, of course, depends importantly upon the assets, earnings, and prospects of the debtors and the *faith* the creditor has in the standing and character of the borrowers.

Accounts receivable and accounts payable, created by transactions of one corporate unit with another, actually total a huge amount at any given time. Although there are no firm statistics available, the amount involved may be larger than the total of the entire amount of credit granted to debtors by the conventional financial agencies of the country. The figure is even more impressive if we include the huge volume of commercial paper that represents the purchase of short-term indebtedness from banks and corporate units by other banks and corporate units. This is a sort of parallel banking system that operates without the orthodox devices. The reasons for the growth in the volume of commercial paper are many, but we are concerned primarily with the fact of its existence and substantial expansion.

Savings-and-loan associations that collect and lend money primarily on mortgages for land and buildings are another kind of mechanism of huge dimensions. The role and activity of this type of agency will contribute to and depend upon the tempo of the building industry, available sources of funds, the interest rates, and the competition by other agencies in the same field. Governmental regulations and restrictions, as well as prices of land, material, and labor, also influence the growth and prosperity of the savings-and-loan associations.

Then, of course, the United States and the British Commonwealth have, for many decades, used insurance institutions as organizations to collect savings and extend credit. Much commercial and residential building construction has been financed by banks, insurance companies and savings-and-loan institutions. More recently, profit-sharing and the pension funds of corporations have contributed to making credit available, particularly for purposes of creating fixed assets both for corporations and for individual family needs; and the investment trusts have made some contribution to the supply of credit.

In lending institutions of all kinds, some of the credit supply comes from depositors, the capital invested by the shareholders (or their equivalent), or the annual depreciation and undistributed corporate profits. And these resources may be augmented by the sale of securities on the financial markets.

Corporations are not alone in husbanding some of their earnings. Individuals, too, create savings—between 5 percent and 8½ percent of their annual disposable income. In the United States, the yearly total of this figure fluctuates around $60 to $70 billion. Much of this sum is deposited in commercial and savings banks, or used for the purchase of insurance, or utilized for the liquidation of portions of debts already accumulated, or for the acquisition of securities, either directly or through one or more of the hundreds of existing investment trusts.

The capital and undistributed profits of commercial banks, too, become a basis of credit if these are liquid enough. In addition, there are two other very flexible credit sources available for use by the banking system. The first, of course, is the right of members of the Federal Reserve system (the nation's central banking system) to rediscount (sell with recourse) a portion of the loans already made as credits by the individual member banks and receive the equivalent amount of credit (or currency) from the central banking agency. Second, the administrative leadership of the Reserve can modify the coefficient of loans to assets and deposits, thereby increasing or decreasing both the base and the actual dimensions and availability of the supply of bank credit.

Some of the restrictive covenants originally placed upon the content of the reserves by the founding legislation of 1913 have since been modified or eliminated. In a sense, the quality of the foundation on which the reserves were first based has changed, possibly for the worse, and, simultaneously, qualitative factors are being given more weight as the bases of our credit structure.

In the exchange of goods and services, bookkeeping, not currency, accounts receivable and payable, not legal tender, are used to complete the transactions necessary to satisfy most of our material needs and desires. When checks based on savings or loans are used to settle debts, the financial process is finally one of resolving, by written order, the residual small balances of debits and credits in a particular bank or among a few banks. Again, currency is not used. The check is usually accepted by both seller and buyer in good faith; and it is discharged in good faith. There is very little clinking of coins and very little rustling of greenbacks attending sale and purchase. The time will probably come when most of our transactions of exchange will be effected by the whirling, clicking wheels and gears of electronic data devices—probably located in some remote centers away from the actual scenes of the transactions.

Faith then, a qualitative factor, appears to be *the* important element in our financial complex. Not only is the United States monetary system truly based upon a fiat medium[1] that draws its strength from what has been, and, it is hoped, will be, a well-placed belief in the future soundness and growth of the United States economy, but faith also has a bearing on the flexibility and of the supply of credit.

Even as a catalyst that converts the potential of a loan into the fact of credit, faith must again play a vital role in the fulfillment of the transaction between borrower and lender. A good loan obviously depends not upon how sound the debtor was in the past, but rather on how successful he is likely to be in the future. The sound loan of yesterday could become the uncollectible debt of tomorrow. A great concept may be a dream in the mind of a man or a gleam in his eye; but if it is valid and is supported by skillful management and a stimulating economic environment, what is a hope and present promise can become a corporate blue chip of the future. The records are full of examples of progressive bankers and other individuals who decided to risk the granting of credit, not so much upon today's or yesterday's balance sheets as on their trust in the human qualities of certain men—their ideas, their plans, their management, their methods, and their motivations.

Thus, it is faith in the potentials and in the growth of the United States as a dynamic body of people that provides the confidence necessary to maintain the *relative* stability of its financial dealings. Upon that faith much of the exchange of the items in the nation's annual gross product of over one trillion dollars rests and rests firmly.

1. Although before 1933 the full convertibility of paper currency into "hard money" was pretty much a myth, after that time it became clear that even paper currency and so-called "silver coins" were no longer exchangeable into their assumed equivalents of precious metal. At present, they are issued by the United States federal government and declared to be, in varying degrees, "legal tender." However, in most instances, each unit of coin or paper money is redeemable by exchange only into exactly the same type of coin or bill as was offered for redemption.

The *demand* for credit, which is the complement to supply in our financial equation, also depends upon many factors and many influences—need, desire, profit opportunities, the confidence of the borrowers, welfare, and social, public, and defense requirements. Growth of population, new products and materials, rising standards of living, rising *real* income, and faith in the future of the nation will play their parts in creating the desire to spend and to make use of credit in order to satisfy today's needs and wants out of tomorrow's earnings.

Faith in the future is essential, not only to the process of supplying credit, but also to the stimulation of its effective demand. If there is general confidence in the prospective performance of a nation's economy—in its components of business, government, and individuals—then debts to satisfy expanding needs and desires are likely to be assumed. If, on the other hand, those same segments of a society are sunk in gloom and pessimism, they are likely to husband their resources and seek to contract rather than expand their demands and their use of credit.

However, there remains a broad spectrum of unsolved mysteries in the sources, uses, and controls of credit. Where does the stream or supply of credit come from and what do we really know about its margins of safe flexibility, its proper rules and regulations? We do know that the rules have been changed substantially over the years and the specifications and requirements governing the supply and granting of credit have been modified just as extensively.

Where does the stream and flow of credit really go as it travels from its many sources to its unknown outlets? Surely the borrower does not really keep possession (except for a very short time and for use in increasing his liquidity) of the actual funds represented by his loans. The credit granted is not locked up in solitary confinement, or in a vault, leaking away its economic potency. Rather it is used by the borrower to pay wages, to build plants, to develop new products, new materials and new methods, to buy more effective machinery, to expand working capital for inventory and/or accounts receivable, and hopefully to earn increased profits. Of the profit, the borrower will pay nearly 50 percent to the government and use 25 percent for new investment in working capital, plant and improved machinery, leaving about 25 percent before taxes for actual distribution, on the average, to the shareholders.

The funds born of credit do not disappear. They only change their form. In a sense, the credits that are drawn upstream from the financial river seem to be poured again into the stream at varying points along its banks to be used again and again.

I wonder whether we are on firm ground when we assume that interest rates, like credit, are the direct and inevitable result of the operation of the simple, long-established, iron-clad economic law of supply and demand. If supply and demand are very flexible, then in relying on them as the definitive causal factors of money rates, are we not busily engaged in measuring a rubber sheet with an elastic ruler? Supply can vary and so can demand; and the interplay of a number of factors will determine the course of the actual relationship between them.

To return to the simile of the stream: if the level of credit is raised by increases in savings, greater profits, and the pull of lessened demand, or by modifications in reserves, then the effect that increasing surge has will probably depend upon the area of demand to which the supply is contiguous. If the surrounding economic environment consists of sterile rocks and barren soil, then the increasing flow will water wasteland

and will have useless or stagnant results. If, on the other hand, the economic environs are fertile and the human workers active, imaginative, and confident, then the flow of credit can be fully employed in expanding production, service, and social betterment. Moreover, this phenomenon will continue as long as the optimism is buoyant and the stimuli are generative and regenerative. With the happy spiral of prosperity or boom, the pressure of demand upon credit will probably be toward higher rates.

If, however, the equilibrium between demand and supply is not maintained, and excessive inventories accumulate, a time must come when there will be a break in the continuity of the economic spiral as consumption fails to equal production. Then there may be a pause, a mini-recession, a full recession, or a depression, until adjustments are made and new stimuli regenerate the progress of growth.

So, too, the economic trends themselves can desert their accustomed paths. When that happens, the yellow flag of possible changes ahead becomes visible on the economic road. Consumer goods and services are much more marked by inertia than are nonconsumer items. People are loath to reduce their standards of living and do so only under strong and long-lasting economic pressures. They do not immediately suspend their patterns of living at one end of a yo-yo; relative affluence will begin to modify their life-styles only very gradually.[2]

In a sense, the inertia of the economy parallels the inertia of consumption. Forecasts of the future made by laying an old-fashioned ruler on a graph of past figures and projecting those into the future are often as sound as those made by complicated reasoning or intricate computer calculations.

2. The author presented this point of view in his previous volumes.

Departures either above or below the line of historic trends often presage an inevitable correction back to the very projected line determined by the humble ruler.

Therefore, it may well be that when demand for credit gets out of line by exceeding the facts of history, the pressure of demand for credit upon its supply will increase; and with it so might the scale of interest rates.

If this thesis is valid, then credit should be controlled not by a law that may have little specific application, but rather by a council of dedicated and open-minded men who will objectively watch all relevant developments and impose the kind of selective controls that make for safe growth and reasonable stability in the economy. Or perhaps these wise men would have to meet regularly in séances with a professional medium to unravel the credit mystique. But whether council or a medium, he should rely on the *qualitative* characteristics of credit.

4.
The Sad Saga of Inflation

Rampant inflation must be rated among the primary economic scourges; but stable prices are no guarantee that all will be beer and skittles: The span of 1922 to 1929 was among the most stable periods for prices in the United States—except in equity securities. Nevertheless, it ended in the deepest and longest depression in the nation's history—running from 1929 to 1939.

It was held by the late Professor Sumner Slichter and others, that modest inflation of prices was on balance a favorable condition, conducive to full employment. However, it is generally agreed that rampant inflation exerts a corrosive effect upon the economic well-being of a nation and of most of its citizens. It erodes confidence in a nation's fiscal stability in both international and domestic markets. It diminishes the purchasing power of bond interest, and of pensions and social-security payments, and the value of *real* wages as differentiated from *dollar* wages.

To the public, persistent and excessive inflation has become a major menace. Politicians, unhappily, too often analyze it from a partisan standpoint. Its real causes are truly verboten subjects—blame is assigned assiduously, but not always accurately. Although there is an overwhelming consensus against radical inflation, there is anything but agreement among economic students as to its causes or its cures.

Not too long ago I met a polite young man who was an expert at the probing interview. We covered a good deal of the waterfront, from A to Z, and when we reached "I," *inflation* was ticketed high on the list of social and economic problems. I was challenged with the remark, "You have lived a long time, seen a great deal, and should be able to tell us what we can do to cure the problem of inflation."

I agreed that I had been around a long while and seen a great deal, but I said that inflation was not one of the problems I had solved. But the remark caused me to think much more about the possible solutions.

It occurred to me that certainly in medicine and perhaps in economics, finding the cure for any disease—influenza, cancer, inflation, deflation, or just "flation"—really depends upon an accurate diagnosis of the causes of the ailment. Is a cure for any of the tragic ailments that have been visited upon mankind ever discovered until the causes are determined? It would seem reasonable to assume that the same approach would be the only valid one to the problem of inflation.

What are the main or basic causes of inflation? Many causes have been nominated by groups with special interests. Unbalanced governmental budgets are high on the list of candidates. Imbalance in world trade and excessive availability of credit and its handmaiden, the injection of money into the economy, are also pointed to as the villains. Then there are many who believe that escalating prices are caused by a lack of equilibrium between what is paid for products and services and what is paid for "the true basis of values," by which they mean gold. And not infrequently, profits, or specifically "excessive profits and profiteering," are blamed.

In various places and at various times there are different causes for inflationary price spirals. Where the value of the currency in the hands of buyers is far in excess of the value of the goods available, competition for the limited supplies will result in premium and escalating prices.

Some inflationary spirals reflect a complete loss of faith in the medium of exchange. The specter of a currency without true or stable value has loomed occasionally, with terrifying effect, throughout history. In some European countries (especially Germany) during the 1920s, the intrinsic value of paper money practically vanished as housewives waited hourly to receive their husbands' ascending wages and rush to the shops and markets to translate the depreciating paper into goods for which the posted prices were also being changed every hour. Depreciation of currency, particularly when it was combined with scarcity of goods, can result in fantastic increases in prices and disappearing values of money.

Of course, there are other bases for greatly escalating price levels. The exchange rate for a nation's currency might be drastically discounted in the world markets due to a severe imbalance of trade. If a nation were dependent upon imports to a degree, say, of 30 to 35 percent of its GNP, and its currency were selling in world money markets at a substantial discount, then the domestic prices of the imported goods would obviously rise considerably. The rise and the lack of confidence would develop a weakness that would feed on itself and create short-selling of the currency, aggravating the problem still further. This was the situation in some European countries, particularly after World War I, when they were short of capital and also required large imports of raw materials and foodstuffs.

Generally speaking, with some dramatic exceptions among foodstuffs and fuels, a scarcity of products has been rare in the United States economy. The industrial complex of the country has usually created a supply of goods equal to, or even in excess of demand at any given time. In fact, so productive is the manufacturing sector of the United States that it ordinarily created a supply that equaled demand and, at the same time, contributed substantial millions or billions of dollars of inventory to the nation's stockpiles. Even during declared and undeclared wars, the balance sheets of the United States show an augmentation of the items of inventories amounting to several billions of dollars annually. In brief, inflationary trends in this country rarely have had their geneses in scarcity values of goods stemming from shortages of wanted items. However, within the recent past there have developed a number of instances of increasing scarcities of vital products in the United States economy. The confluence of short supplies and expanding affluence has placed almost unprecedented pressures on prices and rising inflationary trends.

Conventional economics usually attributes inflation to fiscal and monetary mismanagement. The list of suspects is long indeed. It includes governmental deficits, extravagant governmental expenditures, imbalances in international trade, too large a flow of money into industry and commerce, easy availability of credit to business, and other factors.

Several of these charges are valid. I could argue and probably prove, at least to my own satisfaction, that governmental deficits can be inflationary; but there are also times when they exert a stimulating effect on sales and production. Higher taxes and higher interest rates may also raise prices and thereby prove inflationary—unless they serve, by the bites they take out of the economy, to act as a significant deterrent to the growth of the gross national product and induce either a plateau of activity or an actual recession.

However, the fact that over 70 percent of the total price structure of our economy is directly attributable to past and present labor costs would suggest that wages and productivity are two fundamental ingredients in the inflation recipe. A wage rise of 5 percent that is accompanied by an increase of 3+ percent in productivity will result in little, if any, escalation in price trends. But a wage increase that averages (including fringe benefits) 7+ to 10 percent annually, while the improvement in productivity hovers around 2 percent or less, will practically guarantee an average price increase of 5 percent or more annually. Moreover, I have insisted for over three decades that the base of the economy of the United States was shifting rapidly from production to service and consumption.[1]

The shift of emphasis from production to service and consumption is of more than academic or intellectual interest. Service and consumption as economic forces are far less volatile than production, and an economy based primarily on them is likely to be more stable. On the other hand, production is much more sensitive to the introduction and greater use of mechanical and automated devices. Therefore, an economy based chiefly on manufacturing can largely offset the increasing costs of wages and their inflationary consequences through more intensive investment and the use of more sophisticated manufacturing devices. The effects of high hourly wages become diluted if fewer and fewer manhours per 100 units of production are continually required. To automate service and consumption, however, is much harder,

1. This was discussed in detail in a number of the author's books starting in 1928.

and as dollar wages increase in these areas, it is less feasible to offset the rises by increased productivity. Inflation will occur much more quickly and fully from the impact of rising labor costs in consumption and services than in production.

This does not mean that services and consumption are not being mechanized and automated. However, the area for application is much more limited and the possibilities for increased productivity are more circumscribed.

The only formula that will enable the United States to maintain the world's highest level of both dollar and real wages *and* the production of goods at prices that can compete successfully in foreign markets is productivity and more productivity. If United States labor is to survive in free world markets, it must produce the largest quotient of production in return for the greatest package of take-home pay. For this purpose, the so-called labor-saving devices, often labeled the enemies of the wage earners, are truly their savior. Through the alchemy, very high wages and reasonably low cost per unit of output can exist side by side.

It is on the subject of inflation; principally higher taxes and interest rates, that I disagree with most academic economists, bankers, and government officials. I see tax increases as deflationary or reflationary only if they act as a deterrent on the economy and cause a reversal of the trend and policy of full employment. That approach, it is assumed, would die aborning as a political miscarriage. Increased interest may well *aggravate* inflation because it is a cost that can be added to prices. Only if—a big if—higher interest rates served (as taxes might also) to erode business prosperity would they act as anti-inflationary devices. That alternative would not be a welcome gift—whoever or whatever the donor was.

However, there is one possible consequence of both higher interest and higher tax rates that could apply reverse English to the movement of the economic cue ball as it is propelled by the thrust of Congress. If an increase in interest and/or taxes did serve to deter investment in capital equipment, its effect could be quite the opposite of what its champions hope for.

Let us assume that capital costs, higher because of escalated interest and/or taxes, discouraged the introduction of more modern machinery. Either total costs are likely to increase or employers would seek to prevent wages from increasing; but there is less room for lower prices when profits decrease. In fact, a scarcity of production could develop if the natural forces of expanded demand and capacities reach a point of diminishing return. Such developments would exert no anti-inflationary pressures on prices. Instead, a drought of capital that prevented factory mechanization from proceeding would, in the long run, contribute to higher prices, a poorer quality of goods, or less money for wage earners and shareholders. Thus, the growth of capital investment, by providing for increased production and productivity, is an antidote to the venom of inflation and its blockage is, in the long run, a stimulus to inflation.

To control inflation, we must go back to its basic causes and modify one, or several, of them. Wages are a larger single ingredient in price than profits. Therefore, to control prices, wages must be controlled. Or, preferably, increased productivity should be encouraged, promoted, and enhanced. Then, in order to control inflation, wages and changing wage rates should be gauged by the actual variations in productivity as well as the cost of living. On the other hand, it is possible to affect inflation positively and probably dramatically—but temporarily—by modifying demand and, to a degree, by controlling profits.

The federal and local governments of the United States

spend over $400 billion a year—an amount almost one half as large as the combined GNPs of the nations of Western Europe.[2] Of that amount only a portion, although an important one, is subject to the administration's and Congress's will and decision. If expenditures for welfare, for space development, and for defense, for example, were decreased, the economic tempo would be significantly slowed. Employment would probably decline and the competition by the government for funds would be modified. Under these circumstances, inflationary pressures might lessen, but as a collateral effect, there would be a marked increase in unemployment and other evidences of a recessionary pattern. National income would probably be substantially reduced.

However, reduced government expenditures are not the only instruments for cooling off an overheated and inflated economy. It is possible to conceive of a situation in which prices, wages, and profits are set within predetermined levels by the government. While the excess-profits-tax law has twice been used in modern times to control profits, and, in World War II, an Office of Price Administration (OPA) fixed the prices of practically all goods and services sold, there has never been an effective control except exhortation. A Churchillian appeal in words had the power of one or more nuclear bombs, but there has been only one Churchill in our century. And there was certainly none in the United States during the days of economic price control.

The demand side of the economic equation unquestion-

2. The figures used here to represent total expenditures by federal and local governmental agencies have included transfer payments. These represent subsidies, grants-in-aid to state and local governments, and chiefly, social-security payments (previously collected from employee and employer). It is difficult for me to find validity in the present statistical system of omitting transfer payments from government spending totals in the national income accounts.

ably creates a continuous upward pressure on the price of goods and services. That demand is huge in the United States, where there is an annual disposable income of over one trillion dollars. It flows from the earnings of nearly 85 million men and women who are employed at both high dollar wages and high real wages, as compared to the wages of the rest of the world, and to the prices of items they buy—even though prices have substantially escalated over the past few decades.

The government, too—both federal and local—is a contributor to the flow of expendable and expended funds. This is particularly true when government agencies spend more for their requirements than they collect from the taxpayers. Generally, government deficits add to the pressure of demand by actual or potential purchases without contributing much, if anything, to the supply side of the equation. Here, by the way, is an instance in which monetary factors do play a direct role in the economic or material relationships among people.

Governmental deficits are likely to be inflationary, particularly in periods of full employment, because they inject into the economy more purchasing power and more actual purchases than they siphon out. However, even without creating deficits, expenditures by the government are important both qualitatively and quantitatively. Funds spent for space exploration and moon trips may be desirable, but their expenditure leaves less for education, urban renewal, poverty amelioration, air and water conservation, air terminals, railroads, and improved mass transportation.

For most of the last three decades, the United States government has operated with large deficits, and it is likely that this fact has contributed not only to the inflationary pressures on the economy at home, but to the erosion of the world's confidence in the prudence, good housekeeping, and wise fiscal and economic management of the colossus of the West. But deficits do not always create inflationary pressures. When demand for goods is sluggish and below the level required for maximum effective production, the creation of purchasing power through deficit operation may serve to lower both costs and prices.

In international trade, if deficit financing creates a lack of confidence, it will aggravate the country's problem of the balance of payments and exacerbate other international currency difficulties. The balance of payments will be adversely affected as contracting exports sold at high prices in the world markets erode the total of the nation's trade. The drop in exports will result in pressure not only upon the international exchange value of a country's currency, but also in a reduced volume of domestic production, greater unemployment, and smaller profits.

Do wages follow prices or do prices tag along after wages? As in most of the hen-and-egg sequences in the quasi-art of economics, the label of cause and effect cannot be assigned with exactitude. The presumptive evidence supports the theory that prices usually—but not always—follow wages. The two factors have an intimate interrelationship that years of history have underlined as inescapable.

It is both natural and understandable that the profits of business in the United States should be the target of the verbal darts of labor leaders and their champions, but these critics are mistaken or confused in the semantics and in the arithmetic of their argument.

Let us look at the decade of 1960 to 1970, for example. From 1960 to 1965, prices were relatively constant, increasing only 6.5 percent over the half decade. Wages over the same period rose 34 percent. Nevertheless, corporate profits advanced 74 percent. The reasons for the dramatic increase in profits with a minimal rise in prices lay both in the huge development of productivity offsetting higher wage rates, and in other cost reductions derived from the rapid expansion of sales volume and the growth of automation. Profits, therefore, obviously can grow rapidly in a period of relatively constant levels of wages and prices.

From 1965 to 1970, the picture of the first half of the decade was reversed. Wages increased over the period a total of about 52 percent; prices increased 23 percent, or an average of 4½ percent per year; profits *decreased* in total dollar figures by 11 percent. These facts of wage and price increase and profit decrease developed in spite of a growth of the dollar volume of gross national product by about 24 percent.

Unquestionably the profits of industry and commerce do take their toll of the nation's economy and add to the prices paid by its citizens. However, the approximate dimensions of the costs are measurable. Over the years, about 10 percent of the gross national product goes into the profit-before-taxes column. Therefore, although the percentage may remain constant, the total will increase as the economy grows. To stop at that point, however, would be to misrepresent the facts.

Out of an annual gross national product of over one trillion 200 billion dollars, 10 percent does amount to a colossal sum. But that total presents a very false picture of the profit business takes out of the economy. Approximately a half of the so-called profit is paid to the federal and local governments every year in taxes.[3] That would leave less than

3. If, in calculating the distribution of profits, shareowners' personal taxes were included, the take by government would be increased to about 60 percent; labor would be the beneficiaries of 25 percent (less taxes); and the shareholder would receive, after taxes, 15 to 18 percent of total corporate profits.

5 percent of the GNP. Then, of the $50 billion or less of profits remaining after taxes, another half is invested by business in new or enlarged facilities or held for additional working capital, leaving approximately 26 percent of the original pretax profit for payment of dividends—which will, of course, be subject to additional income taxation. Even this is a sum not to be denigrated, particularly by the shareholders. But it represents less than 2½ percent of the gross national product, and can hardly be *the* or even *a* determining factor in the pricing formula. On the other hand, the proportion of prices resulting from expenditures for either current or past labor is estimated at over 70 percent of the total.

Unless it is very limited in degree and impact, inflation promises no salubrious ending. However, because of the particular nature of the economy of the United States, inflation may carry within itself its own antidote, at least in some measure.

Although psychology rarely changes the direction of an economic trend either downward or upward, it can augment the speed and duration of trend lines, once they are established. When deflation is under way, the attitudes of people determine the severity and the duration of the downward spiral. And when the economy strikes bottom and turns up,[4] psychology will again have a tremendous effect on the speed and the extent of the recovery. Pressing the panic button, and an aura of fear, can wreak more havoc than the disaster itself.

---

4. The economy will make a turn from a decline to a rising trend only when production and commercial activity operate at a level below that which the demands of consumers, producers, and merchants establish as their minimum requirements or when some new stimuli arise.

If the people of the United States dread inflation but are unwilling to grasp its nettles firmly, then what lies ahead? Here we enter an area of conjecture. However, certain threads may be unraveled from the tangled skein. If taxes or other presumed deterrents do slow expansion and improvement of capital assets, then the creation and installation of new products, new methods, more intensive and sophisticated means of mechanized and automated production may be halted. The fruit of that tree will be the rotten apple of a slowdown in our total growth, a dearth of newly created products, the disappearance of competitive prices in world markets, and an aggravation of our problem of combining high dollar wages with low production costs.

If, on the other hand, we place no impassable roadblocks in the way of capital expansion and improvement, the business leaders of the nation will continue to learn to live successfully with higher and higher wages if more effective selling and more automated production are permitted to cancel out a substantial part of the increased labor costs.

The accumulation and dispersal of inventories are one of the keys to the level of business activity and also to both inflationary and deflationary trends in the price level. Projecting certain raw facts of the past into the future, we may assume that United States business will continually repeat its historical patterns in the handling of inventories. These reach very large volumes, sometimes increasing in value as much as $16 to $17 billion a year. However, when the arithmetical increase exceeds a yearly rate of $12 to $15 billion dollars, a powerful—even irresistible—pressure seems to force the total inventory figure to retreat to its historical limit.

The reasons for this oft-repeated phenomenon are difficult to pinpoint, but certain serious and costly risks are inherent in the accumulation of excessive stock. Close to the top of the list is the high cost of carrying inventory, which is reflected in prices. Studies indicate that the cost of carrying inventory in the present economic environment averages over 16 percent annually.

First, there is the cost of capital tied up in stocks on hand, capital that could be earning a high wage in some other employment. The total figure for cost of money tied up in stock is probably around 8 to 10 percent annually.

Second, there is the cost of storage space and facilities. This direct or indirect cost of capital has grown in recent years into a very respectable figure.

Third, if inventories are stored and handled by modern automated warehouse facilities, the capital cost will be markedly increased.

Fourth, laborsaving devices notwithstanding, there is still a need for some labor, and it is paid on a continually escalating wage level.

Fifth, there is always the problem of cost of spoilage and breakage in stocks warehoused for long periods of time. In addition, unhappily, the losses from pilfering by both outsiders and insiders escalate the cost of maintaining inventories.

Profit may accrue from the maintenance of large inventories during periods of continuously inflating price levels. On the other hand, time may erode the price levels or render obsolete or shopworn large parts of the usual inventories. Therefore, although the fluctuations in inventory volume can be a controlling force in short-term trends of the economic cycle, in the long run, inventories should be no larger than are necessary to maintain efficient production runs, to adjust to seasonal requirements, and to protect against discontinuity in either the availability of raw material or component parts or in the supply of the finished goods.

The total United States inventory is now worth more than $195 billion. The cost of carrying this hoard of goods is great indeed, averaging over $30 billion annually. However, the need of adequate stocks-on-hand should not be minimized. The proper balance between use and availability will be of increasing interest to United States businessmen. It is to the improvement of the utility of inventory for good selling, the protection of the corporation from undue risks, and the reduction of the costs of storing, processing, and maintaining adequate-sized inventories that electronic data processing contributes so much, and promises to be of even greater service in the future.

Effective control of inventories can save 16 to 18 percent annually for each dollar of reduction and preclude losses on items that prove to be unsatisfactory. A controlled inventory is less subject to gaps that result in breaks in the continuity of the production process, or in the loss of sales due to failure to have wanted items in stock.

It is conceivable that government, labor, business, and banking will someday join forces to plan sound economic policies and inject forceful and valid constructive states-manship into the economic affairs of the nation.

Someday the federal and local governments may design their tax structures with more equity and fewer loopholes. Perhaps tax collecting will be intelligently simplified so that the costly army of inspectors and collectors that now man the IRS can be replaced by a smaller, more productive corps. It is even conceivable that true capital and current expenses of governmental bodies will be separated and presented independently, measured by different criteria and controlled by totally dissimilar concepts and approaches. Then capital assets that are long enduring may be amortized over periods consistent with their useful lives by the assessment of taxes for the annual costs and depreciation of their total value. The problem of government deficits will then take on a completely new aspect. The real public debt surplus or deficit will then be manifest and subject to better understanding and management.

Over the years, the United States has given in grants for civilian and military aid to other states of the globe, amounts totaling over $140 billion. Perhaps the world, or the Western part of it, has now reached a turning point in the need for gifts from the United States and for the flow of capital for military succor or "conquest" by United States "industrial imperialism." Many of the once war-ridden countries are now well along the road to peaceful success and prosperity. Our friends and former foes in Europe and Asia appear to be fully rehabilitated with new machinery, prosperous trade, and revolutionary agricultural methods devised and exported by public-spirited United States institutions. Perhaps the *means* by which the gifts are made should now be revised.

If, for example, all loans or grants were given with *some* interest charge—no matter how minuscule—they would not lose their aura of generosity or be replaced so soon and so often with gratitude as "a lively sense of favors yet to come." Moreover, if all grants in the future were made, not only with some minimal interest attached, but also with a provision that made them in fact a demand loan or one with periodic maturities—either of which could be exercised or changed at the discretion of the United States—then the present situation in the international markets might be improved. It is strange, indeed, that the money marts and the central bankers should post warnings and sound alarms regarding the weakness of the United States dollar when the weakness is due, in part, to the unparalleled largess of this country in aid, the use of its raw materials in wars, gifts, loans, and investments. If the United States had the power to demand payment, its international financial position would be substantially improved.

Perhaps for the benefit of the world as well as the United States, the time has come to put into effect a reverse Marshall Plan. It is estimated that, at present, there are about 80 billions of Eurodollars held primarily by foreign central banks. This huge sum is loose to slosh around under the varying influences of the winds of trade and rumor and to hurl its mass and might against any weakened currency walls that seem exposed. It serves, also, to stimulate the pantographic effect of those who hedge to protect profit and those speculators who destroy in order to make a profit. At present, that mass of dollars cannot be liquidated except over years of patient and constructive effort. It earns no interest and chiefly creates unrest and even panic in the world's money markets. That huge 80 billion dollar float might be funded into a bond issue carrying low interest rates and extended maturities.

But unlike the original Marshall Plan which had neither interest nor repayment requirements, a reverse Marshall Plan should pay for its keep and repay the principal of its debt.

The monetary problem is soluble because the difficulty of the elements in which, in reality, it exists, are subject to diagnosis, treatment, and resolution.

PART II:
SOME ANATOMY OF OUR ECONOMY

5.
Ingredients of Stability

The state of our economy is due, always, to a combination of forces. Acts of nature, government, and men all exert their influence. Government plays a very important role, and nature is even more controlling; labor and management are also most important contributing factors. But the judgments, decisions, and acts of the men and women who make up the nation are a force that wields the greatest power of all in influencing our material well-being for better or worse.

The possibility for error by a business leader is as great as for a person in the public sector. After all, the official may have been only recently recruited from the ranks of private industry. The difference lies in the fact that the area affected by an error in private enterprise is far more limited than the area affected by an error in a governmental activity. A serious misstep by a public official may imperil the safety, not just of a corporate unit, but of the entire nation. When the policies of a national leader are foolhardy, the nation, perhaps the world, risks catastrophe.

Individual corporate units are like independent laboratories in which economic judgments may be tested and the results recorded. Governmental units are so amorphous that their limits and responsibilities are difficult to determine.

But despite the spottiness of the diplomatic and economic policy of the United States government and of some of its domestic fiscal and business procedures, it has contributed not only to the material well-being of its own people, but also to the people of an important part of the rest of the world. The miracle of United States productivity has occurred in an environment created by both nature and government, but developed by the labor, machinery, and management of competitive industry.

It is likely that the accidental (if accidental, it is) marriage of efforts of government and competitive enterprise has produced—economically, at least—the best system in the world. This does not mean that the best is perfect; far from it. Nor does it mean that the material achievements of the nation are the proper goal and destiny of man. But the combination of forces that exists in the United States has provided the men and women of this nation with the highest standard of living of any country at any time. The mixture of public and private activity is probably a stabilizing force in the economy. Within a nation where over one-third of the GNP is controlled by public agencies and two-thirds of the employment depends upon consumption and services, the volatility—so striking a part of the production cycle—is muted by the less variable motion of the rising and falling of the tides of governmental economic activity.

I believe that the likelihood of another 1929-1933, or more accurately, 1929-1939, depression is very small. Elements of stability are built into the present economy. Under even extraordinary circumstances, governmental expenditures are not likely to move drastically up or down, but usually only up. Services and consumption also appear, historically, to be relatively stable in character. Levels, once adopted, quickly become part of the pattern of living, and when a particular standard of living is attained by a family, retreat from it will be made only under the impact of a truly enormous force and compelling necessity.

The growth and increased use and utility of electronic data-processing equipment have also helped to stabilize business. Today there is a much greater awareness and understanding of the facts and the significance of whatever affects business than there was two decades ago.

However, to assume that the days of recessions and depressions are over for all time is to assume too much. But there is reason to hope that the former periodicity will be ended, that the "bad years" will be farther apart, and even that the profiles of future recessions and depressions will be shallower and shorter than those of the past.

Which segment of the economy is mainly responsible for its status, its control, and its progress? Is it the *public* sector that determines the duration and course of prosperity and recession? Or is it the competitive sector? Here again, in this vague area of the "science" of economics, there is no basis for a definitive answer. However, it is my own unequivocal judgment that the *private* sector, not the *public* sector, determines the course of the economy, at least in the United States.

It has been said that the economy of the United States has become so large that, although the decisions and operations of the nation's governments may affect it within limited areas, they cannot determine its basic course or destiny. Moreover, the expenditures for public purposes—whether wise or unwise, good or bad—are more or less rigid. Public budgets do not decline; only the percentage of increase and the area of spending are subject to modification.

However, besides the apparent fact that the governmental sectors fulfill a role of junior partner in the economy of the United States, it is doubtful if all the thinking and judgment upon which decisions affecting the economy are based are infallible. The programs that are suggested to promote the economy or to dampen it and reverse the inflationary spiral are similar in their nature and in their results. Generally, they concern monetary and fiscal devices and controls. Sometimes a few short-lived exercises in exhortations to business and labor and banking are added. But in practice, without exception, whatever the purpose and whenever used, the measures taken have ranged from partial adequacy to almost total inadequacy.

The reasons may be many. Certainly in the past few years, higher taxes and skyrocketing interest rates have apparently been ineffective. On the contrary, they may have had an effect opposite to the one planned and intended.

The intricacies of what sophisticates include in *their* economics are literally out of the orbit of the men and women whose daily lives and material relationships actually make up the warp and woof of the economic fabric. Within the United States there are over 200 million men, women, and children whose needs, desires, feelings, and actions actually determine the ebb and flow of the economic events of the nation. They may read about the price of an ounce of gold, or about an increase in the supply of money, or the escalation of interest rates—but the reality of these phenomena is very distant from their daily requirements or affairs. Their chief concern is how firmly established are the ingredients in the formulas of the prices they pay and how they relate to the incomes recurringly available to them.

Neither do I accept the thesis, often advanced but hardly documented or proved, that consumers have little or no voice in deciding what supplies will be made available to them. The proponents of this view apparently believe that the economy consists entirely of production and is thus an organism in which the control is held by the corporate managements of a few oligopolies who meet in secret sessions and decide what goods will be made available to the impotent consumers, and at what prices.

It is impossible to make this conclusion jibe with the incontrovertible fact that nearly 70 percent of the United States economy is composed not of manufacturing but of consumption and services. In this segment of our economy, oligopolies have little or no say as to what will be offered by the thousands of large and small businesses that make a multiplicity of goods and services available for the free choice of the people. Moreover, to a much greater extent than applies to a democratic country's government, what is demanded in the market place is a matter of absolute free will, decision, and action. Every day the consumers of the nation cast their votes with cash or indebtedness for the purchase of goods and services. And woe betide the members of the mysterious inner sanctum who have misjudged the quantity, styles, prices, quality, material content, or even colors of what is placed on the shelves. Dangerously increasing inventories, interrupted production, and declining profits will be the fruits of the bad seeds sown by any mistakes of the oligopolists.

The charge is frequently made by critics of the United States economy that its growth and development are too often built upon nondurable bases, that the nation has structured its development upon economic Seidlitz powders that fizz and foam but have few lasting qualities. They point to the phenomenon of so-called "built-in obsolescence," particularly in regard to the automobile, that automobiles become obsolete either through changes in style or rapid deterioration of operating quality. It is claimed that the buying public is forced or *persuaded* to turn in old cars for new ones with the improvements of the new model.

If this were true we would find ourselves confronted with an astonishing statistical phenomenon. There is, in the United States, a total of over 95 million passenger automobiles. In each of the past ten years the number of cars purchased in the United States, including both domestically and foreign-produced units, averaged about 8 to 10 million. If "built-in obsolescence" prevailed, and automobiles lasted only one year, the annual production should have reached the astronomical figure of 95 million cars. That figure is obviously absurd. If "built-in obsolescence" meant junking or disposal of a car even every *three* years, then production would amount to about 30 million units annually. A five-year car life would mean a 19-million annual production.

But the actual annual production has averaged between 8 and 10 million cars. If we add together the losses by fire, wreckage, and theft, we would discover that, as a nation, we have an annual requirement of several million cars. And if we assume that the new families created each year buy proportionally the same number of automobiles as the older families, there would be another increased annual requirement. That would leave a replacement figure that would be subject to a truly free expression and exercise of will and purchasing plans of about 7 to 8 million cars out of the 10 million produced annually. This lower figure really measures the number of cars that must be replaced either by obsolescence or by depreciation and normal mechanical deterioration. If we divide the total actual car population of the nation of 95 million by the average annual requirement due to wear and tear, we reach the astounding figure of not one or two years, but possibly ten or twelve years as the probable average life of an automobile.[1] It may well be that the average automobile passes through the hands of two or three generations of owners, both here and abroad. If the modern car has obsolescence built in, it is also extraordinarily durable.

One to three million people apparently elect to keep their cars for no longer than one to three years either because they believe that early replacement represents true economy or that it offers them the best and most modern product available. That decision is their own affair, and it is not the business of the self-appointed shepherds of the human flock who would protect their "wards" from the risks of their unguided or misguided conduct.

The dangers of polluting the air and waters have been exacerbated from the merely serious to the critical and near catastrophic. The pollution problem has been long in the making, but it has recently spread like a virulent epidemic from a limited area to almost global proportions, and automotive vehicles are among the chief offenders. Many recommendations for the alleviation of automotive pollution have been put forth; several have been strongly urged. Among them are recommendations for the replacement of the present type of internal combustion engines by new kinds of motive power that would create very few or no pollutants.

1. No differentiation is made because of the significant number of foreign cars imported into the United States over the past ten years. The percentage represented by their total is not sufficient to modify my conclusion. Moreover, there is no evidence that the average longevity of the imported cars is greater than that of the domestic product.

How feasible these suggestions are is difficult to determine. How long it would take to produce a revolutionary unit, free of serious faults and as useful a source of energy as its predecessor, must be someone else's guess.

If that is the road to be traveled, however, just think of the impact of this type of obsolescence upon the economy. Millions or billions of dollars would be required for new research and design and for the production of new facilities. Over 95 million automobiles and over 20 million buses and trucks would have to be junked or converted rapidly into units that would meet the new requirements. Perhaps it would take up to ten years, or even longer, to produce enough power units and/or vehicles to replace today's vehicular population.

I have used the automobile as an example to carry the burden of a firm and enduring conclusion about our country. What is true of the automobile is true of a broad gamut of economic phenomena. The stability of our economy is due in large part to growth, and growth comes from progressive and constant developments. Without factors that contribute to change, progress, and improvement, the likelihood of sustained growth is minimal or nonexistent. And if there is no growth, it is doubtful indeed that over the long run there would be, in a nation like the United States, true economic or political stability.

6.
Partnership of the Private and Public Segments

The contributions made by the government to the advancement of new techniques, new materials, and new products, through expenditures for research and development in the fields of space and defense, have combined to give the United States a large lead over most of the world. That margin is shrinking as other nations become more alert and more experienced, and they profit from the aid granted by this nation.

Confrontations on the domestic front appear to have lost their revolutionary quality in an active political or belligerent sense. They involve the conflict between young and old; the battle of the campuses; the real or fake war between the sexes; the struggle between black and white citizens over rights and privileges; the claims of the undernourished and underprivileged; the protests against ecological damage; and the efforts of many groups to advance, often unilaterally, their particular causes. Altogether, a large number of embattled crusaders daily gird themselves to go forth and fight for their rights.

Protest is the proper device for indicating dissatisfaction with the established order. The United States, as a nation, was born out of protest. But protests that are only ferment or revolt, and offer as programs merely a vacuum, serve no constructive purpose. Generally, only if protest is accompanied by plans for progressive changes will it serve a useful purpose.

There is no doubt that much, very much, remains to be done by the current generation to improve the American society which has been granted in trust, not in perpetuity, what is still the most miraculous productive mechanism in history.

This affluent society is not the creation alone of the present generation, but came from their forebears; it belongs to youth to hold for a lifetime and to transmit, in an improved state, it is hoped, to those who follow them. This generation carries the responsibility of safeguarding the principles of universal access to life, liberty, and the pursuit of happiness. And if there is to be more to distribute, more must be produced, not only for the needs of this nation, but for other parts of the world.

The problems of disequilibrium, of inequities in social justice, must be solved by the application of brains and brawn and not by invectives or bombs. There is no value in replacing the imperfect with something worse or with nothing at all. The need is not for slogans and recriminations but for solutions that come only by dint of constructive and intelligent effort.

Government participation is at present an important factor in many of our nation's activities. Space and defense are not the only programs supported by taxes: funds for urban renewal and pollution control; agricultural experiments; welfare and unemployment payments, whether based on today's or tomorrow's programs, all finally must be financed by taxes. The taxes will be imposed upon and paid not by the indigent, not by the unemployed, not just by government employees, but principally by the people who are producing the products and services and profits of the nation.

The research and development of new techniques, new designs, new materials, and new products—which may have been born and may have spent their infancy in the lying-in wards of the laboratories of defense industries—may also spawn products used primarily in peace efforts and developments. A nuclear bomb is suspect as a social and humane tool, but nuclear technology is increasingly used in advancing medical and biological knowledge. The nuclear power plant of "Rickover's" submarine, both before and after development of the Polaris weapon as an integral part thereof, is a mobile offensive and defensive instrument that promises the possibility of "dreadful parity" under almost all anticipated probabilities. But the nuclear power plant promises to become a most important source of energy for the production of electricity! The future holds a far more useful fate for atomic power than propelling all the present and promised fleets of nuclear submarines.

Governmental expenditures in other areas can also greatly benefit the private sector. The construction of dams saves many lives, hundreds of thousands of acres of fertile soil, and millions of dollars worth of food and fiber crops. The water stored behind them during times of plentiful rainfall protect the soil from erosion and make water available in times of drought.

The public expenditures for roads may be a subsidy for the automotive, trucking, and oil industries; but they also enable people to withdraw from the overcrowded, overtrafficked, and overpolluted cities, and to live without either the fact or the temporary sense of isolation that living in the country, or even the semi-country, formerly imposed.

Agricultural research, maintained at public expense and conducted by governmental experts, has contributed much to the productive power of the farmer, to the food supply of the United States (and many other countries), and to the quality of the diets available. Hybrid corn and new types of rice are disease-, rust-, and drought-resistant and produce much higher yields per acre. Government-financed experiments in animal husbandry have created new breeds and more efficient conversion of feed into milk, meat, and eggs. Institutional expertise has also protected the public against the introduction of harmful substances into the diet of poultry and livestock—substances used to foster more rapid growth in the animals.

The ailing, if not moribund, railroads will probably recover if the experimental work now finally being done (in large part by government subsidy) to build and test new types of railway rolling stock is successful. The railroads are by far the cheapest and most efficient way of transporting many types of goods and most commuters. For people who travel between the cities and the suburbs for working and living, the rails afford the best roadbed for quick and economical transportation; the cost per passenger-mile is only a fraction of the same unit cost of car travel. High-speed transportation to and from airports is needed now, and in the near future it will be a dire necessity. Improved railroads promise the best means of satisfying this need.

The economic area that is influenced by government policy and action also includes the fiscal and monetary sectors that are controlled by public agencies and that, at least, greatly modify the trends of volume and prices. Both the monetary and the fiscal economic schools claim that the government, and particularly the Federal Reserve system, has an almost despotic power to determine the course of prices and the vitality of competitive enterprise. But, in fact, the effect of governmental action, though it is indeed not to be ignored, is almost always subordinate to competitive enterprise. The partnership of the private and the public segments endures, even in monetary matters, but the citizens, not the government, finally determine the course of events.

In the potency of the fiscal and monetary policies of the nation, the partnership, or interrelationship, of the public and private segments is both viable and visible. Governmental agencies have much to do with banking reserves, rediscount rates, and the trends of interest charges. However, the true effect of the monetary and fiscal forces on the economy depends *primarily* upon how they are used by the business institutions and the consumers. The supply of money and credit may appear to be a fixed, measurable quantity, but its force in the economy will depend upon the search for and the use of funds by the private segment, and the speed with which the funds are transferred from one private sector to another. That determines velocity, which is at least as important in the public and private partnership as volume.

The threads of a so-called developed economy are so intertwined that it is practically impossible to disentangle those of the public mechanism from those of the private sector. The competitive segment draws a part of its genesis and some of its promotion from what the government does.

All that the government does is financed by the productive portion of the economy or by borrowing. A given activity may be constructive, but it is finally supported overwhelmingly by the taxes collected from competitive corporate units and private individuals. Whether the money distributed by the public agencies is for unemployment payments, welfare benefits, police and fire protection, educational services, roads, sewers, sanitation, bridges, or tunnels—the projects must be underwritten in fact by those who, in the last analysis, pay the tax bills.

It is right and proper that social benefits should be promoted and expanded as broadly, intensively, and rapidly as possible. The clarion call has been sounded for more and more "proper development" of the economy and for less and less chrome and "built-in obsolescence." But eliminating the "chrome" could diminish the actual size of the entire economic pie, and even a generous slice for "public good" is, after all, only a slice. Instituting all the benevolent social programs advocated could be not only dangerous, but catastrophic if, in the process, a serious setback occurs in the growth and progress of the private segment of the economy.

If design, production, and distribution are actually changed by the economic evangelists, a new type of economic religion could develop in the United States. If installment buying, for example, were actually discouraged, the result could be much higher prices and lower profits from a reduced volume of sales. Chrome may not please everybody, but it pleases millions. Installment buying costs the consumer in finance charges; but it has made possible the huge volume of consumers' goods that carry large price tags.

It is the mass volume of business from all its sources that has produced the miracle in the United States economy of high wages, relatively low prices, and reasonable corporate profits and dividends. It is the combination of corporate profits and high individual wages that produces the taxes that create about 90 percent of the annual budgets of all governmental agencies in the United States. Proponents of public spending should keep in mind the *sources* as well as the destinies of the annual income of the country. Although it is desirable to examine and modify the degree to which the public interest is taken into account, we must remember that against the more than $400 billion annual expenditures for public activities, there remains over $800 billion in the GNP that is a measurement of the size of the private sector. It is unlikely that public expenditures will ever exceed private expenditures, but perhaps we are now close to the viable margin of difference. There are already more than ritual grumblings against the tax burdens that exist.

If that concern is valid, it is time to examine what is being done to keep the national breadwinner—competitive industry—active and well. Truly we live during a time when a soul-searching is direly needed by both the public and the private sectors of the economy.

7.
Some Dissection

The combination of means of high productivity with efficient methods of mass distribution created a miracle of production and consumption in the United States that has no equivalent historically or geographically. The credit does not go to the country's fiscal and monetary policies but primarily to the people—what they have created, what their needs are, the modification in their desires and life-styles by imitation, communication, and by all forms of education.

Money and currency, their esoteric terms and properties, consume a great amount of the thought and time of economic experts. The business sector of the nation, including management, labor, consumers and shareholders, is rarely informed about the manifold mutations of gold and credit and money in circulation, and seems to be even less interested. Nevertheless these segments of the population, through their decisions and acts, create the supply of and demand for goods, and thus the state of the economy, which may fluctuate from prosperity to depression.

Analysis of the economic history of the United States indicates that the nation has almost always solved the problem of producing enough to create the supply necessary to meet or even exceed the demand. The astonishing fact that since 1947 the national output in units has more than doubled while the number of workers directly involved in production has hardly increased at all, attests to the productive power of the manufacturing complex and of the techniques it has developed.

The same history, with its recurring periods of excessive inventory accumulation preceding periods of decreasing production to allow for absorption of excess stocks, makes apparent the necessity of increasing demand to support the capacity to produce. The phenomenon of excessive supply has occurred even during periods when demand has been overstimulated by wars and governmental deficits.

In short, just as the mechanical devices of trade are less important than the human factors involved, so the production side of the equation is *less* a problem than the elements that create the total actual demand for goods and services. This does not mean that United States manufacturers are not due great admiration and respect. But it does mean that the methodology of production has outpaced improvements in distribution and in the services.

The most important factor in an economy is its human content; the natural wealth of a country is not paramount. History, from ancient times to the present, is filled with examples of nations whose standards of living remained extremely low while their rich natural resources lay dormant. And currently the two most rapidly growing modern economies belong to countries that are poor indeed in energy sources and in mineral and even agricultural wealth. Germany and Japan, since World War II, have made giant strides in their industrial progress and economic growth in spite of limited natural resources.

The true wealth of a country is the attitude and spirit of its people. People with a will to produce, with the intelligence to create and develop, and with a desire for better lives for themselves and their children are the real foundations upon which the structure of economic progress stands.

A growing population will provide more mouths to feed and more bodies to clothe and care for. But if rising production does not keep pace with increasing population—does not in fact exceed the birthrate—the standards of living and of health are bound to deteriorate. That is not just an academic possibility. Under the pressure of exploding populations, large sections of the world today are suffering declining living standards at the very time when the productive mechanism is expanding.

A country with a growing population that is able to augment production enough to satisfy the growing requirements, is likely to have a growing economy. Of course, if those requirements are limited to the stark needs of food, clothing, and shelter, the country may remain a backward society—economically.

The modification of demand by the creation of desires for more than the brute necessities changes the supply-demand picture radically. Diets that once consisted primarily of carbohydrates will be expanded to include proteins. Food bills will increase, and manufacturing of processed food will become more costly and complicated, but children will grow taller and healthier. The switch to menus that use proteins by way of processed and preprepared foods calls for mechanization and labor in processing the products, but requires much less work in the home.

Agriculture in the United States has converted to intensive

mechanization and has increased yield by using new types of seed and pesticides, herbicides, and chemical fertilizers. The result has been increased productivity per man-hour to many times its base a century before. Fewer workers are necessary to feed more consumers better; and prices at the farm have in the past been kept at a relatively low level, considering the escalating costs of the machines and the services related to them.

Changes in population statistics are one of the less important elements in the demographic trends of a nation. Households and household formations overwhelm in significance and strongly determine the effect of population changes. Practically all consumers' durable goods are requisitioned, not for the individual, but for the household. The house, the car, the television, radio, and hi-fi are parts of the demands of the family. Furniture, floor coverings, air conditioners, refrigerators, freezers, plumbing, washing machines, stoves, dishwashers, and heating equipment are among the many needs or desires of the household. These exist whether or not the family includes one, two, six, or twelve children, or none at all. The total budget for the expenditures demanded by new households and, to an important extent, even by old ones as well, adds up to a monumental figure.

However, the impact of household formations upon the economy is not limited to the demands related to the self-contained requirements of an individual family. For an aggregation of families, the effect is even more dramatic. As family formations multiply, they augment already aggravated situations—good, bad, and neutral. They create the need for sewers, streets, utilities, police and fire protection, and finally for cleaner air and water and more remote living—for retreat from the overcrowded urban centers.

The satisfaction of these new demands of the family has changed the residential map of the United States from a highly concentrated urban pattern to a design, not just away from urban complexes, but toward decentralization into suburbia and exurbia. As new areas of home locations developed, the economic consequences multiplied. The new communities included not only new homes, but services and appurtenances that are their essential concomitants. Roads, sewers, and public-service facilities were followed by schools, churches, and shopping centers. Later, small industrial plants and, particularly, research laboratories found their way near to the new areas of living and the new markets of skilled employees. In addition, the demand for automobliles was enormously stimulated by the need of many families for another car.

As a qualitative factor in the development of decentralized living, the general adoption of the five-day workweek has had a great impact on the economy of the United States, on the amount and nature of the goods and services demanded by the residents of the new areas, and upon the total volume of the nation's annual trade. I was an early advocate of the shorter week.[1] Its impact on the economy and the demand side of the equation has been much more far-reaching than has any of the fiscal, monetary, or quantitative measures adopted over the past three or four decades. It changed the living pattern of the average U.S. family, particularly the role played by the father. It created a totally new concept of "leisure" time and of what products, activities, and services are necessary to occupy the newly available time.

In *The Dynamics of Economic Growth* (Prentice-Hall, 1965), I referred to the possibility of a four-day week. I was neither a proponent nor an opponent, only an advocate of careful, objective study. I maintain that point of view. One plan currently being presented provides for a week of four

---

1. The five-day workweek was discussed and recommended by the author in *New Roads to Prosperity* (Viking Press, 1931).

10-hour days. Assuming a lunch period of an hour, plus another hour traveling to and from work, the total time involved would run from 12 to 13 hours for each of the four days. Then, of course, the studies made of the effects of long periods of work upon fatigue, health, and efficiency must be considered, unless it is assumed that a subsequent step will soon be 8 or 9 hours of work for each of four days, or a 32- to 36-hour work week.

The 1970s present an economic profile very different from that of the 1930s. When, in 1931, I proposed the adoption of a five-day workweek, there were unused production capacities, *depression* levels for the economy, and large reserves of practically all types of unemployed labor. At that time, the decentralization of people and businesses was potential rather than real. Subsequently, our economy expanded spectacularly to create enormous new demands. Automation was born in the forties and, after World War II, grew rapidly to supply needs and desires. Rising manufacturing productivity and more extensive requirements for services stimulated jobs and fulfilled the magic formula of high wages, reasonable prices, and full employment.

Automation will continue to expand, but probably at a slower rate. Changes in the living patterns of men and businesses will become far less dramatic. And with a four-day, 32- to 36-hour week, the shortage of labor for the full use of a complicated production complex may prove wasteful and conducive to higher costs and prices. The recent movement for a three-day workweek, if successful, might spell even more rapidly rising costs and prices and thus result in constantly declining standards of living.

If the proposed plan of four working days each week specifies 10 hours per day, then capital assets representing huge investments would be unused for three days. Of course, if the workweek were 4 days of 8 or 9 hours each, the labor shortage would become drastic; the pressure for overtime and moonlighting at 1½ or twice the regular rates could greatly escalate labor costs and therefore prices. There remains the unlikely possibility that we shall "normally" have a substantial reservoir of labor to use our capacity fully.

The short workweek will create special problems for the *service* segments of our economy, where a 4- or 3-day workweek cannot promise increased hourly productivity—services make minor use of automation to increase efficiency. Moreover, services are likely to require constant availability—not for 3 or 4 days per week, but for 7.

Nor can the managements of service organizations determine the schedules that consumers will insist on setting. They want household equipment, for example, serviced when the need arises, not between the hours of 8 and 10 A.M. or after 6 P.M., but when the housewife or her representative is likely to be at home. And in retail service, the patterns of buying by consumers are not equally spread over a 10-hour day, but are concentrated between particular hours on specific days. These buying patterns could be at odds with the working hours desired by the employees. A three- or four-day week for the worker could, and probably would, mean either substantial overtime and overworked labor or an undermanned facility for segments of the desired shopping and service portions of every week. As much damage can be done by the bad timing of a good idea as by the good timing of a bad idea.

A workweek that is shortened by cutting an hour or an hour and a half off each day, rather than by reducing the number of days, will do little, constructive or otherwise, to change the pattern of living for families. It will have almost no effect upon demand—regardless of what it does positively or negatively to production—except that it may escalate prices, and therefore reduce real wages through shrinking the purchasing power of the dollar.

Changes in life-styles may have their origins in causes other than new living areas and new schedules of work. Even though there are at present too many families in this country whose income condemns them to substandard levels of living, there are four times as many households whose incomes allow them not only the necessities, but also some of the luxuries of life. However, what began as a luxury can eventually become, as did the automobile, radio, and television, almost a necessity.

The flow of new products that has its headwaters in the laboratories and on the drawing boards grows into a production stream that empties continuously into the marketplace. A high percentage of the commonplace articles of consumption of today did not exist two or three decades ago. As private and public research-and-development efforts and expenditures have increased the supply of new ideas, new materials, new designs, and new products—the markets have been galvanized into greater activity. And the consumer has been educated or influenced or even titillated into a more active desire for products and services. Some people are critical of this persuasion, seeing it as an unwise appeal to greedy appetites. Others say that if the new had not been assiduously hawked at the expense of the old, the world would have stagnated at the preindustrial stage.

Research and development are big business, not only in products for defense and offense, but for the peacetime market. They are joint efforts of government, industry, and technical organizations, a pattern that may change in the future under the pressures applied to our educational institutions.

The American citizen's sense of deserving the best the economy has to offer may stem from the philosophy upon which the country was founded. "All men are created equal" may be a hope rather than a fact, but the urge to live as well as one's neighbor and to provide that the next generation shall live better than the present one is a spur to ambition. Only one boy at a time can become president, but the many true Horatio Alger rags-to-riches stories are evidence that this society is not crystallized or stratified.

The American corporate philosophy is unlike that of the European of the past. American industry does not base its approach to pricing and wages on a predetermined profit or dividend rate. Profits and dividends are, rather, the residual, after competitive pricing and wages are established and a portion of the profits is allocated to improving or enlarging capital assets.

One result has been a constant upgrading of methods and the development of more sophisticated productive mechanisms. Another has been a constant improvement in the quality of product and an increase in productivity per man-hour. *Relatively* reasonable prices have accompanied reasonable profit returns on both sales and capital investment.

Since World War II, as a result both of the export by the United States of capital in the form of gifts and investments, and of improved management techniques, many countries in Europe and Asia have been able to adopt our methods.

Other stimuli have helped to develop and expand mass distribution in the United States, including overt advertising and the covert exposure of people to design, to fashion, to travel, and to new products. Billions of dollars are spent annually in paid publicity to create new desires and demands and *more* desires and demands.

Financial devices have supplied explosive energy to the

mass markets for the products of mass production. The invention and development of installment buying, or "fractional selling," has probably done more to stimulate consumption, and therefore production, than any other fiscal or financial mechanism. Consumers presently borrow nearly $130 billion annually to purchase goods and services. Practically every commercial bank in the United States lends money for consumer buying, either on installments or as loans to be amortized later.

Currently, 50 percent of the automobiles sold in the United States are bought on the installment plan, as are large percentages of the television and stereo sets and the household appliances. Even clothing is sold on the basis of payment over a period of time. And services like trips and airplane transportation are now offered on an installment basis.

Whether or not using today's items that will be paid for tomorrow has an adverse effect upon morality and encourages profligacy must be decided by those with greater wisdom than mine. In any case, it cannot be denied that installment buying (or fractional selling) has had an enormous economic effect, with *qualitative* as well as quantitative economic results. The device has expanded the market for big-ticket items from hundreds to thousands to millions. The huge markets have furnished the volume upon which the mechanization and automation of United States industry have been built. The minute division of labor necessary for utilization of machines is profitable only when the total volume of production is immense. Low-cost mass production is tied to mass distribution.

If any event interferes with the continuity of *production,* there are usually banks of inventory sufficient for some time. But if the flow of goods through the channels of distribution into the consumers' hands should be stopped, or even reduced, the effects would be dramatic, serious, and rapid. Inventories would quickly accumulate, production would be cut back, and reduced employment and higher costs and lower profits would result.

That is one reason why I regret the unilateral "half-truth" approach to the so-called "truth in lending." There can be no objection in principle to telling the truth, if it is the whole and not a half truth. The consumer who uses credit should be aware of its costs, just as the producer should be aware of the costs to him of carrying inventory. Many items go to make up the costs of consumer credit, but the cost of borrowing capital, including compensating balances demanded by the banks, now amounts to nearly 9 percent. Other costs include losses, bookkeeping, collection charges, deterioration of returned purchases, etc.

What are the probable effects of a successful campaign against credit costs? If the effect on the buyers is negligible, then a great many motions will have been made to little avail. If it reduces the charges made for credit to the consumer, it will be beneficial, provided of course there is now an attractive margin of profit for the lender who offers consumer credit. However, in our highly competitive economy, the fact that variations among credit charges are minute would indicate that the profit margins are not excessive, or even substantial. (This excludes the profit on the additional sales made possible by installment buying, or fractional selling.)

But let us assume that the so-called "truth in lending" decreases the volume of sales based on consumer credit. Then if the cash sales do not increase accordingly, the total volume will contract. If the relatively low costs in the United States derive from huge sales, any substantial decrease in the volume will affect costs adversely. A loss of 10 to 20 percent of a market could raise costs and prices more than that. The net result could well amount to little or no saving of interest charges for credit, and a large increase in the total costs, and therefore in the final prices paid by the consumers.

To sustain full employment, the volume of manufacturing must increase almost continuously. As the sophistication and productivity of the factory complex raise output per man-hour, more sales are required to maintain and augment the number of man-hours usable. The phrase "imperative of growth" has become so commonplace as to be platitudinous. But so are "clean air," "pure water," and "nutritious food." Without growth, pure water, and clean air, we would face disaster. Without growth, American standards of living would certainly deteriorate, and the grapes of economic prosperity would sour or wither on the vine.

Growth in the United States is not only beneficial but essential. As the demands of the public segments increase—an incontrovertible historical and probable future fact—financing them will inevitably create either a welfare state or an enormously larger competitive economy.

PART III:
THE ROADS TO GROWTH

8.
Economic Growth: Its Genesis and Nemesis

Economic growth is the generally accepted criterion of a nation's material well-being. But there is less than general agreement as to the means by which growth can be attained at home or abroad. Nor is the passage of time instructive as to what factors underlie economic growth.

Proper planning and handling of the tax program, which will in turn influence capital investment; control of credit, or interest rates, or the volume of money introduced into the economy; adherence to the gold standard; balanced budgets and favorable trade surpluses; self-restraint and psychological discipline by business units and individuals—all have their advocates. The list of supposed stimuli is almost inexhaustible; the evidence of their efficacy is inconclusive and unimpressive.

The failure of a society continuously to modernize the design of its products and programs will guarantee a lack of progress and lack of growth in the economy of the society, whether it is large or small. The living patterns in such a society will remain static, whether the year is 1574, 1974, or 2474. Many tribes live on our globe untouched by the progress (or retrogression) of modern civilization; their morals and manners have not changed for hundreds or thousands of years. For these people there is little if any economic growth. There are no new designs, no new products, no new methods. Theirs will remain a primitive society regardless of time.

Growth requires new products and new designs to create and to fulfill new consumer desires. New desires and new products require better and more efficient means of production—greater productivity by the social group as a unit and by the individual and the corporate producer. Increased production will supply the increased demand.

To convert the potential demand into augmented consumption through a greater volume of sales, purchasing power must be increased. This means that an important share of the results of production and productivity created through advanced techniques must flow to wage earners so that they can afford to be more active consumers and thereby absorb the expanding supply of goods and services. This does not mean that labor can safely take more than its fair share; if it should, there will be little incentive for investors to provide the necessary financing. Capital, too, is entitled to a fair and proper return, or rent; in fact, it will demand one. The risks and lack of return on investments in borderline industries, particularly in countries whose economy or political stability is precarious, often deter capital investments, in spite of the promise of theoretically high returns. Only some probability of safety, along with a fair return, attracts capital.

For continuous economic growth, relatively high money wages are necessary. But high wages are useful only if they represent real wages and real purchasing power. Real purchasing power depends not only upon the rate of dollars paid, but also on the productivity of the worker. If the formula of merging high wages with reasonable prices through the catalyst of high productivity should be adversely affected, the price to the nation, its workers, and its industries could be high. Some other countries have populations as large as or larger than the United States. The population of China, for example, is about four times as large. Nevertheless, China's economic growth has been pitifully slow. It will remain so until it has learned and put into practice the lessons of high productivity and high real wages.

Management as well as labor may oppose the introduction of laborsaving devices or sophisticated methods of increasing productivity. In many countries, the failure to maintain progress in capital installation was due to the myopia of executives. The competitive urge for modernization was always strong enough to impel action until it was too late. Unions have sometimes believed that modern productive complexes tend to eliminate jobs. By no means, however, have all labor leaders seen automation in this light; the late John L. Lewis of the United Mine Workers Union was in the forefront of those who encouraged the introduction of laborsaving devices.

But when labor and management have cooperated, they have often instituted programs for avoiding loss of jobs by those already employed. Labor has also sought a very substantial portion of the savings resulting from the purchase and operation of sophisticated, more productive, and much more expensive manufacturing mechanisms.

But if the present trend of wages continues, and if every possible effort to introduce highly automated and complex production methods is not made, the result must be further erosion of the position of the nation in international markets and of real wages in domestic markets, and economic stagnation for the country.

The service industries have become the senior member of the economic triumvirate: production, government, and services, and the total effect has not been entirely benign. Is it feasible to apply to the service activities some of the techniques so successfully worked out in the mass-production complex? Would it not be possible to organize segments of the service industries so that they could adopt some of the methods used in manufacturing? For example, the costs of building homes and factories have increased greatly. This increase is partly due to high interest rates, increased land prices, and the mounting cost of materials and labor. As most of the work of fabrication is performed on the sites of the completed structures, there is little opportunity to offset the greater costs by increased productivity through sophisticated and automated production methods.

There are three possible devices for avoiding or offsetting part of the escalating costs that are making the sale and purchase of building structures, for dwelling or working, less attractive. The first is to enlarge and intensify the "do-it-yourself" method of constructing simple living units, such as modest vacation houses or extra rooms. There are hundreds of thousands of men in the United States who are reasonably expert in the use of building tools and who could put together precut lumber, ready-made window frames and doors, packaged insulation and exterior and interior wall-board and roofing, simplified plumbing and heating and electric wiring systems, easily installed air-conditioning units, and the other necessary ingredients. Varied plans and specifications are already available. And even the materials are offered in increasing supply in building-supply supermarkets. Those to whom a hammer or a saw or electrical tools are not a threat can eliminate on-site labor costs.

Second, there are plans for mass-producing prefabricated home units containing plumbing, heating, and air-conditioning within a factory-made core, with the outside shell in modules that, when assembled, will surround the basic mechanical heart of the home. Thus, there is at least the prospect of using mass-production methods to create, at more reasonable costs, a complete dwelling unit.

Third, there is the mobile home. This is built in a factory as a bus would be; it is a dwelling unit on wheels which can be moved behind an automobile; it is ordinarily not transferred frequently from one site to another, but is moved to a particular location and there perhaps removed from its wheels and anchored more or less permanently, with attachments to outside electric current, water lines, and sewer facilities. The cost per room or per square or cubic foot of the mobile home is substantially lower than that of the conventional dwelling unit constructed in place upon a permanent foundation and basement.

There is also the possibility of a revolutionary new method of an insured annual payment for construction workers so that the impact of high labor rates will be softened without loss of total income to the individual worker.

Then there is the entire array of household appliances and automotive equipment—the total number of which grows annually—each of which regularly needs servicing and repairs or periodic maintenance. The present system requires a serviceman to visit the patient, diagnose the ailment, and give the necessary treatment all at the site—if possible. It might be feasible to design the individual units so that the heart or core of the mechanism is self-contained as though in a capsule. If the mechanical organ fails, the serviceman could, with minimum effort and in minimum time, remove the unit from its surrounding body, "transplant" a properly working unit, and return the ailing member to the "service factory." There, by modern mass-production methods on an assembly line, the necessary repairs or alterations could be made, and the unit placed in a reserve bank ready for implantation into a new patient. Perhaps this plan is oversimplified or impractical; otherwise, it certainly would have been put into practice long ago. But wherever module servicing is practical, the productivity of the serviceman would be multiplied; his wages would suffer no adverse effects; and the cost and inconvenience to the consumer could be markedly reduced. No doubt many attempts have already been made to design mechanisms with removable operating cores that could be replaced and repaired by modern production methods. However, application of the concept has been limited to only a few of the myriad mechanisms now produced en masse but serviced individually at home or in a repair shop.

If defense spending could be safely reduced, the funds released would be quickly and properly absorbed by the public sector, assuming that the well-being of society and social betterment are essential. First, we need new, better, and more housing for the less affluent. Also, clean and safe streets are not only political issues, but essential to the pride, the health, and even the survival of communities. We need cleaner air, purer water, and edible seafood. These are unsatisfied demands, the fulfillment of which will require an accelerated tempo of economic growth.

As the population of the world in general, and the United States in particular, builds to a probable doubling point in the next generation, the need for all manner of things becomes staggering—among them vast amounts of food.

American agriculture has multiplied its capacity to produce food and fiber many times over, and has dramatically reduced the man-hours required to feed an expanding population. At the same time, in spite of rising levels, it has supplied food at prices that enable Americans to spend smaller and smaller percentages of their income on food.

Nature has helped: there is the rich soil, particularly in the Middle Atlantic, Midwestern, and Pacific Coast states; fine systems of rivers; and adequate rainfall. And farmers have always been willing to work hard for long hours.

Then farm machinery was invented and developed in the United States. Improvements of seeds for crops have been developed by the federal and state governments. Water was brought to dry areas. Then chemical fertilizers replaced the natural basic and trace minerals that the increasing yields of crops took from the soil. Finally, weeds and insects were fought successfully by herbicides and insecticides.

But an alarm was sounded. It was claimed that birds became sterile; fish died or did not breed; that even people were threatened with various diseases. *The Silent Spring* by Rachel Carson became a battle cry. It painted a picture of the country as a desert sans birds, fish, bees—sans almost all things living.

Edicts and laws first were demanded, then became facts. Farmers were exhorted to go back to "natural fertilizer" and away from the "sterilizing chemicals." The fact that the use of "natural fertilizer" or "organic farming" cannot be defended by sound logic and that the use of virgin acreage obviously depends only on the basic and trace chemicals and minerals already in the soils, and not on natural fertilizers or organic farming, carried no weight. But certainly a serious decrease in the feeding of soil by chemical fertilizers and trace minerals would dangerously reduce the production of food for the nation and the globe. And while there is cause for concern about the use of some herbicides and insecticides, eliminating them entirely would also endanger the food supply.

As highways and exurban developments sprawl across more and more of the countryside, there are annually millions fewer acres left for the production of food and fibers, and further intensification of productivity will be mandatory. Flood control, for example, will require huge investments and enormous efforts. The price will be high, but the return will be higher. The need for increased use of chemical fertilizer is a certainty. The argument over the use of pesticides and herbicides must be resolved. We may find ourselves on the horns of a dilemma, one of which is the risk of harming birds, fish, and people, and the other the risk of invasion by disease-bearing insects and pests that may destroy much of the food and fibers that otherwise would be available for the increased demands of human consumption.

The space program, culminating in the trips to the moon, represents an investment of more than $64 billion. It is difficult to evaluate the net benefits versus the cost of this effort. It has unquestionably advanced technical knowledge of space rockets, satellites, and space itself. Original and unique products have been conceived and produced by space technicians. Advanced computers, new batteries, new cameras, new television devices, new food formulas, new metals, and new sources of electrical energy are but a few of the products of the space program. It is difficult to evaluate the effort, judging it against the need for curing cancer, solving problems of poverty, improving housing, air, water, and mass transportation.

Most large urban centers of the United States ache from

neglect, filth, vermin, inadequate sanitation in ghettos that should not exist, and lack of safety and security for all of their citizens. The disease is already advanced and a cure may no longer be possible. The cities exert a powerful magnetic pull on the population of the countryside. Suburbia has begun to take on some of the aspects of the city centers, and the urban districts threaten to spread their ghettos and other problems ruthlessly and inexorably.

Many cities of the United States suffer from unprogressive planning and progressive deterioration, but there is too much value, too much wealth, too much utility in these large and small metropolises to allow their further disintegration. In the renaissance of the cities lies the promise of improved social conditions, better living areas, civil progress, and an enormous stimulus to economic growth.

The development of an increase in the absolute number of the aged may trigger a reverse migration back to the cities. Commuting is not now an attractive prospect, especially for older people, divided between the pulls of the activities of the cities and the seclusion of the country. Nor is the automobile a desirable alternative means of travel.

If the transportation problem is resolved, the marriage of suburbia and the cities may be a happy one. If not, the separation of the two will widen. Solving the problem may not prove to be a stimulus to the economy, but failure to solve it will detract from the well-being of the nation.

The cities could offer expanding and increasingly attractive diversions to their aging residents. The parks—when they become safe—the shops, the museums, the movies, the theaters, the free concerts could become more and more inviting to more and more elderly couples.

But transportation problems involve more than improved rolling stock and roadbeds and better operation of railroads.

The inadequacy of the airline terminals and their mechanisms and organizations is a matter of grave concern. Better terminals and new and expanded means of transportation to and from airports are essential.

New high-speed means of mass transportation must be developed. Super-fast trains moving on welded rails, rapid transit in cars suspended from monorails, and even air-cushioned land and water transports are possibilities for the future.

Capital investment is the cornerstone of economic growth. Laws that stifle it could seriously injure growth and prosperity.

The same warning applies to governmental and other restrictions on the security markets. This does not mean that those markets should not be subjected to constant observation, study, and supervision. It would be best if they could be self-policing, but if they cannot, some governmental agencies will assume the responsibility of protecting the public and the investors. At the same time, those charged with public responsibility should not forget that the tool they are policing is vital to the flow of capital into the American economy, that its growth must not be impeded by a serious lack of funds.

Two characteristics of the role of capital and of financial markets in the United States stand out. As separate forces and in combination, capital and markets are enormously important in the formula of United States economic growth, and the forces that modify them both are not primarily quantitative, but qualitative. True, the evidence of both capital flow and market activity are statistical. But the statistics are merely the sequential phenomena that state the results of qualitative factors that have determined both the state of business and the state of mind of those who buy and sell the securities.

Upon the social and economic topography there is a huge mountain of human needs that demands attention. The choices we are offered include, first, indifference to the existence of the problems; second, the erosion of the mass by the use of a shovel whose capacity is obviously inadequate; and third, an attack with a heroic-sized steam shovel activated with the zeal of earnest endeavor and the power of human energy. Hope alone is not enough to make dreams become realities. But the combined power, brains, and will of the public and private segments of our society should be adequate.

9.
Which Way to Growth?

Quantitative factors *are* important but far less so than *qualitative* factors—people and their patterns and standards of living. Qualitative factors cause 200 million people to act; the forces that flow to and from men and women determine their acts and the course of the economy. The cycle of life of most of these social or sociological stimuli follow patterns that resemble those of biological entities. They are born; they grow; they mature; they deteriorate; and they die, perhaps to be reborn in a different form. And the economy reflects the symptoms of their weaknesses—even their impending mortality—unless a transfusion of new and equally potent stimuli is injected into the economic bloodstream.

Qualitative economic stimuli may be either negative or positive. If negative, they may deter or even paralyze growth. Inadequate air terminals, roads, and mass transportation; unsatisfactory health facilities, substandard educational tools and personnel, substandard housing facilities, and, finally, undernourishment and poverty deter growth.

There is another group of stimuli that we might identify as "generative." They generate a force that varies both in the time pattern of their application and the volumetric power of their impact. These stimuli, which are indigenous to expanding and developed economies, relate first to the demographic factors of a society; then to the pattern of living that mores, education, and the mass media promote; and finally to the commercial and industrial procedures and devices that have developed into generally accepted practices. The power and force of the people of a country, of their needs, desires, and demands are, in advanced economies, awesome phenomena.

Generative stimuli also include public works, which usually become increasingly active in times of a depression. They range from constructive and stimulative projects to raking leaves. Welfare payments and the proposed annual wage (if and when it comes), unemployment insurance and social-security payments also belong to this group. The funds expended for these purposes are usually limited in impact; they are likely to have little, if any, expanded collateral effect and will promote growth only if they themselves continue to increase.

In absolute terms, defense is a substantial item among the generative stimuli. For various reasons, its opponents have exaggerated both the relative and the absolute burden this expenditure places on the economy. If the sum is modified by the effect of inflation, or measured as a percentage of gross national product, the weight of defense costs is substantially reduced and is far less than the relative burden placed upon the economy of Russia. (This is an economic not a political judgment.) Defense expenditures usually contribute to growth only if they continually expand.

But defense expenditures have a ricocheting effect upon

the total economy, as do other generative stimuli. Research and development expenditures, whether in space programs, mass transportation, new electronic devices, or the medical and agricultural fields, may stimulate industrial growth over a fairly broad geographic section—a nation, a continent, or even the entire globe. The generative stimuli may thus become regenerative. This was true of the development of the jet engine and of satellites for communication and for weather observation.

Unfortunately, among economic stimuli one should not omit wars, in spite of all the tragic impact upon human beings and their societies. Wars spend and waste not only lives, but material wealth as well. However, they do increase the production of arms and material, and the rapid consumption that accompanies accelerated usage. Wars have always played a far too important part in the histories of nations.

The balance between the "stimulation" that wars bring and the ghastly prices they impose leaves a tragic deficit as a penalty for the lack of peace. In human and social terms, the cost of war lies beyond the limits of reasonable measurement. As for the economy, man should surely be able to find sane alternatives to conflict.

The third group of economic stimuli are the "regenerative" forces. This group is the most difficult to pinpoint but offers the most dynamic and exciting possibilities. Regenerative stimuli may begin as small nuclei, but they spread over broad areas and drastically change the producing, consuming, and living habits of millions of people.

Regenerative stimuli are the milestones that have been erected by combinations of nature, science, effort, accident, and wise intent along the road of a nation's progress. In fact, they are likely to mark the route of its economic advance and of the improvement in its standards of living. To some, these milestones are devices for causing the deterioration of living patterns from simple and frugal to wasteful, unsocial, and even ungodly. To others, they mean advancement from undernourished bodies and unsatisfied desires to the satisfaction and fulfillment of the individual demands of independent men and women.

George Romney, Nixon's former Secretary of Housing and Urban Development, has pointed out that past periods of great American prosperity can be labeled with the tags of important contemporary developments that gave impetus and stimulus to the economy. He might have cited railroads, automobiles, aviation, or the five-day week.

History has clearly marked many of the monuments that have kicked off past periods of economic growth. The present exists too fleetingly to be captured, and only a few of the possibilities for the future are imaginable. Many regenerative devices and methods were ridiculed at first. But Stephenson's railroad, after years of trial, puffed its way into fame. Fulton's steamboat, Ford's and Selden's horseless carriages, the Wright Brothers' primitive plane, Edison's electric light, the developments of electric mechanics and, later, the electronic media received no blare of trumpets on their introduction—but nobody ignores them now. No doubt certain onlookers strained their ribs laughing at the demonstration of the first wheel just as some people today sneer at the supersonic plane. Imagination has always been central to improvement in man's estate. But by no means has it always been welcome.

10.
From Yesterday and Today Into Tomorrow

Most of the economic avenues we have so far traveled have been either well trafficked or well marked. Some have been already traced on the map of the future. A few still remain part of men's dreams, unmarked and unsurveyed. These last belong in a sense to the "space age" of the economic, social, and scientific developments that may lie ahead. We may now take a short hop by the rocket, satellite, or plane of our own imagination into the wild blue yonder.

Nearest at hand is the very development of space rockets and satellites themselves. Already the scientists, technicians, and astronauts have accomplished within little more than a decade much more than was envisioned even by Jules Verne and H. G. Wells. Both Russia and the United States have sent unmanned satellites into orbit. Some, with men, have visited the moon and returned. Others have photographed Mars and sent back to earth, by television-radio waves, detailed photographs of that planet.

It is not possible for most of us to understand the complex of power, computer, television, radio devices, and the tracking and correction methods used to keep the rocket on course, or the means of protecting the astronauts themselves for the long trips into weightless space. Most of us accept it all as a miracle of scientific achievement. What the ultimate value will be of voyages by men who are no longer earthbound is impossible to imagine.

From the development of satellites that are sent and remain in orbit beyond the gravitational pull of the earth, the pragmatic results are already impressive. We have built and launched the Tiros satellites[1] which return weather information to earth. This information, available to all nations, improves our ability to make accurate weather predictions and may someday help men to control the weather. Satellites designed and built for Comsat and launched into orbits 23,000 miles above the earth provide increased intercontinental communication and international television. Before the use of satellites as electronic mirrors, the short radio waves used for television transmission restricted it to the distance of visual horizons. With the ability to reflect these waves or beams from satellites orbiting high above the earth's surface, the limitations of· ultrashort radio and television waves were surmounted. Messages and pictures have been sent to and from the moon and from Mars, and instantaneous televised pictures and telegrams to and from most parts of the globe have become common. Space and electronic technology are a most likely source of future regenerative stimuli.

Some regenerative stimuli have serious unexpected consequences. Near the turn of the century Park Avenue, from 42nd to 96th Streets in Manhattan, was converted from an open cut for the railroad tracks to a blanket that obscured from the view (and probably the knowledge) of most of

---

1. All the weather satellites were successful; four are still in orbit, others were turned off by NASA.

today's New Yorkers the trains that run below the billion-dollar complex of high-rise apartments and office buildings. That development was extraordinarily regenerative. When the elevated railroad structure was removed from Third Avenue and from the Avenue of the Americas, there was a transformation in the architectural profile of those two thoroughfares. There arose a spate of high-rise office buildings that is still in a stage of active expansion.

But there are *some* collateral consequences of these developments that may have gone largely unobserved. The areas were formerly occupied by many ramshackle, low-profile buildings that housed nondescript tenants and scores of small bistros. Today most of these have disappeared, or are soon likely to, to be replaced with more skyscrapers, housing thousands of day workers and attracting many more thousands of visitors from 10 A.M. to 5 P.M. The former myriad of small restaurants have been replaced by imposing marble or travertine lobbies through which thousands of people trek to high-speed elevators.

The regenerative effect of this expansion of construction has stimulated the city's economy, and perhaps the nation's. But the impact on mass transportation, vehicular traffic, eating facilities and shopping in the area was not anticipated. However, correcting the situation may provide future regenerative stimuli.

More recently, the southern end of Manhattan has exploded into an unprecedented expansion of building, and a revolution in the character of several neighborhoods. Not long ago there was talk about a shift of the financial district up to midtown (above 42nd Street) and some actual movement. Then the Chase Manhattan Bank built a very large complex, with rental space, for its own headquarters on a full block downtown. This *apparently* anchored the financial center to the Wall Street district; the Chase building was followed by other bank buildings in the immediate and nearby neighborhoods. However, the possibility still exists.

These developments in the center of the narrow geographic strip of southern Manhattan were followed by an astonishing conversion of the whole district along the East River from old one- and two-story brick and wooden buildings that housed mostly restaurants and marine-supply stores to high-rise buildings, already erected or planned.

Even the New York Stock Exchange, which was either going to be moved across the Hudson or sunk in the river under the weight of increased municipal taxes, appears to have decided on a permanent residency in Manhattan, in the southeastern end of the financial district. In fact, the new facilities may be built not *along* but *in* the East River. But most of the land in that area was recovered many years ago from the sea, and with piles, fill-in, and modern methods, the construction may be practical.

Across that same narrow strip of land that separates the East and Hudson Rivers, another enormous development has been added. The Port Authority, which runs the district's tunnels, bridges, and air terminals, has built, on a preferred-tax basis, the twin-towered World Trade Center flanking the Hudson River on the former site of the Washington Food Market. These towers are higher than the Empire State Building. The rentable area is estimated at over 9 million square feet. The techniques of building both the foundations and the superstructures are revolutionary and somewhat controversial. The working occupants, it is assumed, will reach a figure of 50,000, and the daily business visitors and sightseers may reach twice that number. This is a new large city that has been constructed in a small segment of the western edge of the nation's largest metropolis.

The impact on traffic will be great. Whether the problem relates to pedestrians, mass transportation, or the vehicular facilities, today's conveniences will prove woefully inadequate. New means must be planned, designed, financed, and constructed. How, where, and by whom remains to be seen.

Then the thousands of people will consume thousands of meals—tons of food—daily. Providing facilities and transporting supplies to a suddenly magnified population will not be easy, and many of the old food-dispensing shops will be obliterated by new giant high-rise buildings that may not provide eating facilities for the hugely increased number of workers and visitors.

People also require living quarters. The choices must lie between seeking adequate transportation to areas nearby and the construction and maintenance of contiguous apartments of fairly high quality and low costs. Community centers with green belts and shopping services would be preferable. For it seems that all of the self-contained characteristics and requirements of a tightly knit suburban center will have been spawned in the midst of one of the most densely populated cities in the United States.

How much planning is necessary to meet the needs of revolutionized areas is problematic. Nevertheless, some planning is mandatory. With adequate planning, new cities and new communities within cities can provide powerful regenerative stimuli. Without it, they can result in disorganization, catastrophe, and even civic strangulation.

Manhattan Island is uniquely a captive of its own geography, surrounded as it is by ocean or river waters on all sides. At present, it is in a straitjacket—a water prison. It can expand only if it continues to grow vertically or leapfrogs the rivers, or encroaches on the banks of the rivers with land-fills.

The problem of the restricted geography of Manhattan seems to be recognized, at least in glimpses. For a long time there have been periodic appeals for the rehabilitation of the

New Jersey flats, which cover 19,600 acres across from Manhattan. New Jersey actually commissioned Paul Ylvisaker to begin work on such a plan, but the complications were burdensome, and the problems seem to have gone back to their pigeonholes in the files of forgotten or neglected projects. However, development of the Jersey flats as a sports, industrial, and commercial park close to Manhattan is now underway.

There are also plans to change the character of Welfare Island, which lies in the East River north of midtown. The plan calls for the razing of the present institutional buildings and putting up apartment houses in their place. The access roads to and from Long Island and Manhattan have not yet been designated, but the plan indicates a far more effective use of the land than is presently the case.

What is happening in New York is happening in many other cities. One example is a project in the San Francisco Bay area called "BART," for Bay Area Rapid Transit, an extensive and exciting service for the commuters of the district.

BART is a 75-mile transportation system, constructed with welded tracks and automated equipment. The initial cost is estimated to about one-half that of the competitive equivalent service offered by superhighways and automotive vehicles. The per-passenger cost and the time required for traveling are also believed to be about half that of car travel. Besides, BART promises to contribute to easier and cleaner living.

Even before BART is completed, its effects as a regenerative economic catalyst are becoming visible. Downtown San Francisco experienced an exciting rejuvenation, and the building boom of the area soon totaled more than a billion dollars. Future economic fall-out is estimated to be far-reaching and of huge dimensions.

The concepts of speed and distance were revolutionized by

aviation. Long-distance passenger travel by train and ship is rapidly becoming a thing of the past. Perishable goods are carried increasingly by trucks and, for long distances, by plane.

Planes, terminals, and access roads are in a continuous state of inadequacy. The changes that the future demands will require billions of dollars of direct expenditures for increased and improved facilities; and the regenerative effect upon transportation, factory expansion, and, probably, housing development will activate even more dollars.

The supersonic-speed-transport plane, or SST, has become an international football. Russia has already completed its own first supersonic passenger prototype. France and England have cooperated in building two or more prototypes, christened the Concorde.

In the United States, already years behind, the tides of opinion for and against a program of supersonic prototypes flowed back and forth for a while. Now the issue has been resolved. Congress has decided that there will be no further federal subsidies for the SST program. In the legislative bodies and the press, and among groups of economists, conservationists, and some scientists, the judgment has been negative.

There were three arguments against the program: First, that the government should not subsidize commercial ventures for private interests. This meant no SST, as no private institution could support the financial burden and the risks involved.

But the principle of government subsidies in the United States is almost as old as the nation. Grants of land were made to encourage private capital (mostly European) to build the railroads. The returns for the original bondholders were indeed dismal, but the benefits that accrued to the nation are a matter of history. Then the public expenditure for road construction—and particularly for hard-surfaced roads and superhighways—gave enormous impetus to the automotive industry, not only in manufacturing, but in the economic and social effects of the service segments that developed collaterally.

Second, there are the ecological risks of supersonic planes, which are the proper concern of public-spirited individuals and groups. Before the SST could fly in numbers that might have seriously adverse effects, years of testing and improvement in designs will be required. But without a prototype, no test, except in the columns of the press and the panels of legislative and private councils, will be available. If the proper safeguards for the public are not worked out before the gates of unrestricted commercial development swing open, they should remain shut. But to lock the gates and throw away the keys *before* an actual test can be made is not logical.

The third and final argument against the SST program concerns its presumed economic effects. The antis assume that the funds that were to be spent for the SST could be as well, or better, spent elsewhere, particularly for more social benefits. But this argument raises a serious question of principle. Funds spent for space projects and defense have a relatively modest factor of multiplication. Welfare expenditures, essential as they are, also have a very low multiplier. Each dollar spent creates little economic activity beyond the original act itself.

The SST program, if unsuccessful, would similarly have very little effect upon the economy beyond the primary expenditures themselves. If, however, the total project proved to be successful, the sequences could be dramatically regenerative. It would protect our airplane industry, already an important segment of our economic mosaic. Then the development of what would, in effect, be a new industry would create new dimensions with many times the size and impact of the nucleus created by the funds spent on the prototypes. These larger sums would greatly augment the amounts that could be spent on social and welfare demands.

The arguments against the SST could have been made against almost any new development that raised new questions. Today the jet engine, for example, is acknowledged to be the best power unit for practically all commercial aviation. But there was a time when resistance to jet engines seriously delayed their development. A few men in the United States army were still crusading for jet engines for United States warplanes some time after German and British planes were already using them. And, although the invention of the jet engine is usually credited to a British engineer, Air Commodore Sir Frank Whittle, his government was reluctant to support its commercial development. Ironically, it was the United States that developed and built the jets that fly the planes of most commercial companies everywhere. More than 80 percent of the planes for commercial air travel are produced by American factories.

Now that supersonic commercial planes have been outlawed for the United States, what will be the results on international aircraft production? Unless all nations prevent both military and commercial supersonic planes from being built or flown, the ecological threat remains, but the market for faster-than-sound planes would be lost to the United States. Foreign supersonic commercial planes would preempt the skies and foreign workers and suppliers would reap the economic harvest from their construction and sale. These planes of the future, which *may* be a serious threat to our atmosphere, will carry the insignia of France, the United Kingdom, or the USSR, or perhaps Japan.

The Pacific is the cradle of the largest portion of the world's population, and the area around it promises to become the most rapid growth zone of the globe. Much of the earth's untapped resources lie within its wide expanse. On the broad stretches of the Pacific Ocean, distances are measured in far greater dimensions than elsewhere, and the increase in speed to shorten time schedules has a correspondingly greater payoff. To maintain its position in economic power, Japan will surely be tempted to develop faster air transportation. It has the facilities, the expertise, and the finances to design, build, and sell its share of the world's SST fleets of tomorrow. The history of the jet-powered plane of yesterday may well be repeated, but to the benefit of other countries.

The decision made by important U.S. air transport corporations *not* to exercise their options to purchase the French-British Concorde planes unquestionably dealt that model of the SST a hard, if not a mortal, blow. Some editorial comment immediately applauded the presumed death of the venture and wrote, without tears, a hoped for obituary on the passing of the "unholy" supersonic "monster."

The "burial," like the rumored death of Mark Twain, may prove to be both premature and a gross exaggeration. The future course of progress and events lies behind the mists of the tomorrows. There is, by no means, any certainty that the continued development of the SST is at an end. There is only the assurance that the *unchanging* factor ahead of us in the future is *change* itself. The history of scientific development guarantees the probability, if not the certainty, of the continuation of the trend of increased sophistication in our material progress. It is most likely that the art of aviation will, in the future (as in the past), continue its program of increased speed, capacity, efficiency, and safety. And the record of transportation from men's backs, to the wheel, the wagon, the train, the car, and then the plane will maintain its trends of more and more speed that shrinks, in time, distances measured in miles.

If research and development work in the United States on a SST were to be revived today, it would probably require ten years before the commercial models would be ready to fly. It surely would take not so much a sage as a foolhardy individual to determine what the dimensions and characteristics of design, operation, pollution, and ecological risks will be a decade in the future. The tempo of change has been and is likely to be so rapid that only an anointed prophet would risk reading the future in stars or in tea leaves.

Part of the British press condemned the action of the U.S. aviation companies which dropped their options for the purchase of the Concorde. They claimed this action was the result of a willful attempt to injure or destroy European plane production. That is both unfair and absurd. The United States is wallowing in a sea of imported products.

It might be of interest to point out that the difficulties which face the Concorde in achieving a more successful result apparently do not relate in any way whatsoever to the specters that were paraded before the U.S. Congress and dragged through the U.S. press. There appears no mention of the problems of the "resulting air pollution" or the sonic boom. The adverse criticism is now outfitted in the costumes of high construction costs due to inflation, inadequate capacities and revenues, and uneconomic maintenance and operating charges.

Unquestionably, the Siamese-twin arrangement that called for models of the supersonic plane to be built *both* in the United Kingdom and in France, increased the total investment and probably juxtaposed each nation in competition against the other to maintain the employment dependent upon the continuation of the Concorde program. Moreover, it is by no means implausible to assume that Europe, with all its rapidly developing technology in the design and production of sophisticated products, is still an "undergraduate" compared to the U.S. postgraduate in the field of commercial aerodynamics.

However, if the Concorde or any other model of a commercial supersonic plane should prove, finally, after a reasonable test, to be inadequate as a base for commercial air travel, then, regardless of any factors of little or no pollution or livable levels of the supersonic boom, the Concorde as well as any other advance in a plane or any other novel device of more modern transportation will not and should not join the ranks of desirable equipment for men's use.

It is undoubtedly true that in the crucible of time, men's ideas that were ridiculed by their contemporaries have nonetheless been tested over the centuries. Many of them have been tried and burned to ashes—but others have run the gauntlet of fire and we have seen the dreams of men and the plans of their imaginations converted into successful realities to satisfy their needs and desires.

Perhaps the supersonic plane will be destroyed by its trials; perhaps it will prove to be truly flameproof and essential as another cog in the wheel of men's progress.

Who is wise enough to prejudge?

But electronics promises to surpass aviation as a regenerative force. The telephone and telegraph, radio and television record-keeping, manufacturing and process control, design, management, measurements, space and nuclear missiles are altogether only a small fraction of the array of electronic devices already in existence. And there is still a huge field of unexplored potential: e.g., instruments for better medical service and diagnosis, for amplified home communication, for consumer analyses, for sales promotion, and for improved knowledge storage and retrieval. Electronics has set off a third industrial revolution, and one that will change our daily lives even more than did those of the nineteenth and twentieth centuries.

Prognosticators cannot foretell the scientific, economic, and political probabilities of the future, nor whether they will be constructive or destructive. If a nation is affluent, it is condemned by many within and without its boundaries for being so. And as for scientific and commercial advances, the enemies of progress condemn them all, including the accumulated good, because they have discovered some harm and some risks. So to fix the roof, they would tear down the whole edifice.

They wage their war against some real and many assumed evils, but their battle against nuclear energy is the most irrational. When man released the power locked within the atom, he opened the door to undreamed of regenerative potential. The promise and dangers of nuclear power must be taken into account in the calculations that men and societies make for their future programs. There are risks in generating nuclear power, certainly. Perhaps the risks are as grave as its critics claim. But it is possible that man, who has learned how to release this powerful genie from its prison, can learn also to control it.

We hear of experiments to untrap huge reserves of subterranean gas and greatly increased supplies of fossil fuels—coal and oil. There is talk of constructing a new canal near the Panama using the power of nuclear energy to create the necessary fissure. Nuclear energy is now used to power submarines. But the most promising and most controversial use of the atom is as energy to create electrical power directly for utilities.

Experts agree that over the next few decades the demand for electric power will at least triple. There are three natural sources of energy for producing electric current. The first used was water power—so-called "white coal." The second was the fossil fuel, coal. The most recent are petroleum products, oil and gas. Water power, particularly in the United States, reached its top limits of utility decades ago. Coal and oil are now the main energy sources.

The use of coal mined in the United States has recently increased, along with its mobility, and its cost. Oil, of course, is even more mobile than coal and is competitively priced. However, both discharge pollutants into the air during combustion. Nor is the supply of either coal or oil inexhaustible. Coal deposits in the United States are estimated as only adequate for hundreds of years, a short period in the lifetime of a nation.

U.S. reserves of petroleum and natural gas are more limited. Petroleum reserves are estimated as sufficient for probable demands over the next twenty years. Twenty years ago they were estimated as sufficient for only two decades. But during that period, huge deposits of petroleum have been discovered and developed in many other countries for shipment to the United States, and to markets formerly supplied by this country. Besides, the technology of refining has improved, greatly increasing the yield of gasoline per barrel of crude oil. Still, with all the effort to improve methods and to develop new sources, U.S. reserves have remained static.

What promise does the future hold—a surplus of domestic crude, a stable supply, or a serious diminution of reserves and huge imports? Will the problems of the tar sands and oil shale be solved and their huge potential supply be added to what appears to be, in reality, a shrinking domestic crude reserve? (Domestic sources are emphasized because, in a world of uneasy peace, there can be secure reliance only on sources within the limits of the North American continent. These, at least, can probably be protected in time of war. Moreover, foreign supplies create an adverse balance of payment.)

Because of the looming energy crisis, the utility world has turned to the use of the atom as a source of energy. The early promise was almost unlimited. Competitive costs for large-scale kilowatt production of nuclear energy, its comparative cleanliness, and the probable future availability of fuel supplies, made it seem possible that the tripled energy demands of the next century could be met.

Electric utilities not only in the United States, but in Europe and Asia, arranged with atoms-for-peace agreements to construct power plants of unprecedented size to create millions of kilowatts and, as a by-product in some cases, the desalination of salt water for industrial and individual consumption.

Then a series of protests, primarily in the United States, began. It was said that the thermal effects produced by nuclear plants destroyed life in the bodies of water beside which the generating installations had to be built to provide a cooling medium for their hot effluents. Cooling towers were suggested as a solution to that problem. But those were said to be destructive of scenic beauty in the summer in all latitudes, and, in the northern areas, ineffective in the winter, as the flow of water down the sides of the towers cooled and either created a man-made fog or a pinnacle of ice that rendered the whole device inoperative.

Fears were expressed about possible air pollution not by gases and fumes as in the case of coal and oil, but by radioactive fallout. Finally, there is the problem of disposing of the used uranium-fuel pellets. It is feared that they would leave a radioactive residue that might be a health hazard for centuries.

The proponents of nuclear power recognize some of the hazards. But they believe that the great benefits of nuclear energy and the critical need for new sources of power outweigh them. The facts for and against nuclear energy must now be measured and evaluated—not emotionally, but objectively. Surely if man has learned how to release the power of the atom, he can learn to control it and to apply it for beneficent purposes. But only men's application and ingenuity and scientific knowledge will find the answers; and only time will tell whether the power of the atom will turn out to be only malignant or primarily benign.

The United States is not the only country now using nuclear fission as a source of electrical power. Although the first successful reactors were developed here, they have been duplicated and put into operation in the United Kingdom and Italy. The needs of those nations for nonfossil fuels as a source of energy may be greater than ours, or the voices of protest less strident. But although the pace of progress may be slow, a greater use of nuclear power is a certainty for the future.

PART IV:
WHITHER THE DESTINATIONS?

11.
Horizons– Clear and Stormy

It should be clear that my theses hold that economic dynamics and growth are dependent upon the number and power of the regenerative stimuli injected into the economy. But the outlines and the dimensions of those catalysts which are available at present and those that lie beyond the near horizons are difficult to delineate.

Nevertheless, both the past history of our nation and future industrial possibilities of explosive forces do indicate, in vague and sometimes even in definitive outlines, many catalysts which give promise of accelerating the pulse of the economy and expanding its circumference.

In the past, there have been scores of reagents—some supplied by public and others by private agencies—which have added their magic potion to the formula to produce dynamic economic growth and improve man's material well-being and standard of living. The subsidies for railroads, for the building of roads, bridges, and dams have used public funds and initiated forces that have expressed themselves in the hugely expanded dimensions of consequent economic activities.

For the future, there can and will be many avenues—some narrow, some wide—that will stretch from today into the tomorrows. The list is long—too long for recital here. But it might serve a useful purpose to survey some of the more patent areas which, in the future, may offer important forces of stimulation for an active and prosperous economy, and, also, a few which promise significant problems that should either be solved or offset by other very positive actions with beneficial results.

The energy crisis which most experts believe confronts the United States is a dramatic case in point. The demand for energy is expanding significantly and ruthlessly. There is a probability of shortages in locally produced natural-gas and petroleum products. The dual results of this dilemma are a need for both expanded and new reserves. There already exists a rapid increase in the importation of foreign supplies of oil and gas (condensed 600 to 1 and transported as a liquid from abroad in specially designed and built tanker ships). The consequence is to increase the tactical risk of depending upon uncertain foreign sources for a large segment of our energy needs. Equally serious is one other result of the large imports of oil and gas. Conservative estimates hold that from this one deficit, under the present conditions of demand and supply of energy, the United States will face, within the next 20 years, an adverse item in its world's trade balance of payment of as much as 25 billions of dollars annually.

Such an excess of imports over exports—if maintained—offers one or more of three choices. First, the United States must devise or develop more and new products and services which will supply an export surplus, to balance, in whole or large part, the import surplus due to the purchase of oil and gas from foreign sources.

Second, new domestic reserves of energy must be discovered and developed. Realistic economic price levels must be allowed for the production and purchase of natural gas in contrast to the present ridiculous condition of importing gas at three times the price that is permitted by the federal government in interstate shipment of the same kind of fuel and energy. Moreover, and third, the requirements of valid ecological standards must eventually measure the risks of excessive protection of the environment against the essential requirements of industry, commerce, and particularly of the people in their essential needs for a good life, high standards, and the satisfaction of their energy requirements for light, heat, air-conditioning, and transportation. Unquestionably, it is desirable to save the birds, bees, deer, and moose. But man, too, is entitled to safeguards for his standards of living and comfort, even if at somewhat lower levels.

To offset the probable negative balances of trade stemming from huge imports of energy, all the factors conducive to expanding exports must be pursued. The United States has lost much of its quasi-monopolistic position in the manufacture of mass-produced goods of excellent design and quality. Nevertheless, as a production complex this nation retains a preferential position in a significant segment of some sophisticated products. In computers and other highly technical mechanisms, the United States maintains an advantage. This advantage must be retained and intensified. At present, this country holds a near monopoly in the production and sale of commercial planes. This must be maintained by research, development, and proper means of producing and selling. Care must be taken that the present favorable trade position relating to the contemporary types of airplanes is not made obsolete and abandoned by the failure to develop and produce the future generations of the units for air travel and transportation.

However, the present domestic energy problem has

reached the level of crisis and requires further efforts. New sources (new areas, oil shale, and oil-bearing sands) must be prosecuted in terms both of the technology and development of those that promise new and prolific increments of supply; and their needs for funds and expertise for research, and later large amounts of capital for commercial development, must be satisfied.

The whole field of nuclear agency as a source of energy should be explored and promoted as aggressively as possible in order to contribute additional needed power and to do this with all possible protection of the environment. Nuclear plants using fission should be developed with maximum emphasis on desirable sites, utmost protection in its design and construction, and superlative safety in the maintenance of every unit built and in operation.

And, finally, all other possible sources of energy, including waste conversion, should be examined and prosecuted as fast as practical and advisable. Nuclear plants based on fission will be followed by breeder reactors. After fission there may come fusion (which at present offers most difficult problems of construction and control), the promises of whose successful operation would include an inexhaustible supply for man's requirements for energy, and operation which would contribute almost a negligible amount of pollution and radioactive residue.

And then, of course, there are other areas of energy that demand serious consideration. The harnessing of the tides has been a possible project for generations. There is, at present, one completed development. However, the program remains by and large in the field of potential projects. The engineering difficulties and the probable cost are enormous.

Gasification of coal at the sites of mines holds real promise of lower costs of producing and transporting cleaner and more flexible fuel than coal in its present form. Moreover, the supply of coal possesses an estimated life span measured in centuries. The program of perfecting the process of its conversion into gas is under active development; but its successful completion appears to be still some time off.

Oil shale and the petroleum-bearing sands of Canada also offer large but potential sources of gas and fossil fuel. Their development and constructive contribution as sources of energy should be accelerated by a combination of public and private cooperative efforts in research and development.

Solar energy unquestionably represents an inexhaustible source of power. But many problems still remain to be solved and the requirements of the space necessary for the solar panels and batteries for storage of electricity created during periods of sunlight are more than modest.

The development and use of fuel cells are intriguing possibilities. These would allow the creation of decentralized units for creating power without expensive cables and dependence on central stations. But their practical application appears to be a long distance off.

The use of energy and power from the geothermal sources of heat from beneath the surface of the earth is demanding increased attention. Presently, the producing sources of geothermal energy are scarce and widely separated. The limitless heat that exists 30,000 to 50,000 feet under the earth's crust may await means of drilling and protecting both shallow and very deep wells, perhaps deeper than those already developed and down to temperatures that offer the probability of melting most metals now in existence. However, this possible and almost inexhaustible supply of safe energy demands active pursuance of research and commercial development.

Whatever may be the future means to satisfy our needs for

energy, their problems and promises must be resolved. Failure to do so would leave us a nation with its industry, transportation, light, and control of heat drastically reduced or even paralyzed. A solution of the energy crisis will allow the orderly expansion of our economy necessary to satisfy the needs of the increasing material standards of a growing population. We have much to gain by adequate answers to our pressing problem. We have even more to lose by our failure to discover and promote proper answers to our difficulties.

Although energy may be our most pressing problem, there are others almost as serious. The voracious appetite of Western "civilization," in peace and war, has consumed a very large segment of many of our mineral reserves—iron, bauxite, copper, silver, and many others. Already, the United States is dependent upon foreign sources for much of its supply of raw materials. And the time will come when our requirements will be satisfied even more by the supply available from beyond our borders. Again the increasing problem of a growing adverse balance of trade rises like an economic specter which can be laid to rest only if we can expand our exports to pay for our imports of products and raw material and find new domestic reserves or new substitutes for the necessary ingredients for our industrial mix.

Then there exist additional problems to be resolved. To fill the growth of our population and transportation requirements we have crisscrossed the nation with superhighways and main and secondary roads. But in a sense we have double-crossed our railroad systems—which are still the only way to transport the bulk of freight economically, and which also serve as potentially the best and cheapest means of transporting our population over short hauls between urban centers and their suburban beds and living rooms.

The basic roadways of the railroads are in existence. Additional new and very expensive rights-of-way are not required and therefore need not be purchased. The cost for each passenger mile is actually, or potentially, the lowest of all methods of transportation. Improved rights-of-way are unquestionably necessary; and revolutionary and more efficient rolling stock, proper consolidation, and good labor practices and productivity are desirable. The need for improvement is present and compelling. The rewards of a resolution of the problem would be great indeed. But the cost of a failure to find proper answers to our transportation problems could be spelled out in the tales of handicapped and moribund cities, isolated environs, clogged roads that act as parking lots, and a retrogressive or even crippled national economy.

Pollution has become a very important segment of our ecological problems. Poisoning of the air we breathe and the water we drink is the result of the production of waste that has grown more rapidly than have the means of adequate attacks upon the problem. As men have expanded in numbers, their own waste products as well as the sewage and pollution that have accompanied the creation of products for an expanding population and the growing demands for improved standards of living have reached critical proportions. Moreover, the intensity of awareness and demand for solutions have written the words of our problems in bold italics. In a sense we have confused, at least to some degree, status and progress. There is no doubt that our present status is unsatisfactory. It has always been so; and it will remain a fact in the future. That is, until status reaches a point of perfection; which is likely to be never. For a glass half full is still half empty. And a receptacle 7/8 full is still 1/8 empty.

If, however, we measure our conditions in terms of progress, then our future appears very different. The scourges of disease which once wracked the globe are in the past. Man's longevity has increased from a span of thirty years to one over seventy. There has been a diminution in the raw sewage and wastes dumped into our rivers, lakes, and oceans from both human, animal, and industrial sources. The belching of pollution and noxious gases from industry's chimney stacks has diminished. And the poisons emitted by 120 million automotive vehicles have been reduced substantially, even if the situation is measured by progress that is not yet adequate as measured against a required scale of an almost perfect status. Much has been done, but much more remains to be accomplished. Again the benefits of proper solutions will allow our historically rising economic material standards to continue their trends. Failure, on the other hand, will impose a tragic handicap and price upon our future material development. That condition may be desired by some; but it is a goal not ardently to be desired or sought by the great majority of our population.

In all the examples that I have presented as factors to prevent degeneration and promote generative and regenerative forces in influencing living standards and economic development, it should be clear that the tasks of research and pilot plant or model development probably should be shared by both the public and private segments of the economy. Competitive industry, even in the United States, is not rich enough in cash resources to finance the necessary research-and-development costs of seeking and finding all the new and better means of discovering adequate reserves of energy, improving present methods for transportation, and obtaining clean air and water. At present, of U.S. business earnings, business spends about 75 percent for taxes and capital plowed back into new or enlarged facilities or additional working capital. The depreciation reserves are, in most instances, consumed, as is indicated by the fact that liquid assets of U.S. corporations do not expand rapidly and often not even adequately, as costs of inventories and capital equipment constantly escalate.

If *all* of the remaining profits now distributed were used for finding improved means of reducing pollution, increasing power, or improving transportation, the resulting billions of dollars annually would prove woefully inadequate. And the loss of all dividends by shareholders would be likely, indeed, to affect adversely, if not totally, the willingness of 30 million stockholders to invest much of their savings in the volatile equities which satisfy much of the capital requirements of the U.S. industrial complex.

It seems probable that in some cases, much of the research and development work of tomorrow's complicated requirements for more and improved products and services must be shared by both the public and private segments alike.

After the pilot work is successfully completed, it can be expected that the huge investments necessary for the development and equipment of industry, commerce, and services with the necessary commercial implementation will be satisfied by industry itself and financed by the retained profits and capital obtained from an affluent body of public investors.

There is another segment of economic factors which offers the possibility of significant, if not huge, increments of regenerative stimuli for the economies of the world in general and the Unites States in particular. This relates to the promise of the opening of the gates to expanding international trade on a scale far larger than history has heretofore recorded.

The year 1972 was probably unprecedented in the extent and intensity of important international diplomatic discussions and agreements. Mr. Nixon broke the barriers of complete isolation which existed for over twenty years between the People's Republic of China and the United States. And later in the same year, Mr. Nixon visited Moscow and, with the leaders of the USSR, agreed upon some limitation of arms, opening of educational and research relationships, and increased trade activities—certainly in the sale of wheat, probably in the purchase of oil and gas, and possibly in the export of sophisticated machinery. Basically, this is a barter deal. But it is my opinion that in the final analysis practically all international trade is based upon barter. Second-guessers may criticize adversely the terms and technique of the wheat deal; but, omitting judgments made after the facts, the transactions seem to have been and to be advantageous to the Soviet people and to the U.S. agricultural segment, and even to important portions of the entire economy of the U.S.

Two-thirds of the world's population lives east of Suez. Japan, the nation which has already risen to second or third position (and promises to challenge seriously Number 1) lies in the Pacific; most of the virgin sources of minerals and other raw materials, as yet underdeveloped, are in the western (or eastern) Pacific.

It seems likely, indeed, that our planet will find, in the vast cradle of humanity and its worldly goods that is the Pacific area, its future center of expansion and power. The United Kingdom has transferred its former expensive policing of the area to the U.S. If we, as a nation, should abandon our present essential role in the balance of power of that area, then the interests that are so importantly held by the British Commonwealth and France will depend upon elements of strength that at present appear frayed or even unraveled.

It may be that the foundation stones laid by Mr. Nixon will prove to rest on sand and will fall from the pressure of destructive forces upon an unstable base. But if the roads of trade and relative peace have truly been opened by recent events, then the promise of a stream, even a torrent, of international trade could well beggar all historical comparisons.

The risks of permanent improvement in world relations are great. But the promise and possibilities are even greater. World trade could be at the threshold of the greatest expansion period of our history.

It should be noted that within this catalog of prospects of the maintenance, development, improvement, and expansion of our economy, there is *not one* project that depends primarily upon monetary or fiscal factors. Most of them are derivatives of man's plans, patterns, decisions, and actions. Whether they are generative or regenerative in character, all of the economic stimuli and catalysts examined stem *not* from computers or arithmetic but from men, their minds, needs, desires, and actions. The overwhelmingly significant forces which will shape our economic future are not *quantitative* in form or substance but *qualitative* in their nature and content. Their results may be expressed finally in quantitative statistics, but their geneses lie in the qualitative thoughts and acts of men.

12.
Beef à la Mode

Among the pieces of unfinished business facing our nation and its people, the problems of food must be given high priority. They encompass not only escalating prices but shrinking supplies. In one sense the situation is not complicated; its apparent complexity lies in the fact that it involves the diets and skills of man, factors of his demands, and nature's bounty or lack of it. Moreover, there exists a very essential, if not always visible, correlation between one segment of the economy and a seemingly unrelated or at least a disparate sector.

After many decades of food surpluses, the United States finds itself with a present and probably a future shortage of feed and meat. Since the 1930s, the federal government has paid subsidies to support falling prices of farm products. Over the years it has accumulated, at its risk, huge crop reserves held in storage.

Now these reserves have approached the zero mark. Land is being withdrawn, no longer from production, but rather from the soil bank; and billions of dollars of annual subsidies are being phased out. Long existing substandard price levels have reached their historical parities and even exceeded them. The changes have been dramatic, their causes multiple.

Nature's climate—its floods and droughts—and well-intentioned efforts of ecologists and conservationists in successfully attacking the uses of herbicides, insecticides, and adequate chemical fertilizers have dangerously reduced supply. A wide and spreading network of roads and a decentralized population have chewed up farmland and filled it with housing developments, factories, and roadways. The very matrix of agricultural production has been significantly eroded.

But that is not all that has taken place.

It was a strange, powerful, and, in many ways, an unhappy concatenation of forces that developed in 1972 and 1973 to influence the supplies, demands, and prices of food and feed. During that period of time, nature chose to be harsh, indeed, bringing storms, freezes, rains, and drought. In many places crops were scant. Thousands of cattle were undernourished and many died from adverse weather conditions. Moreover, in some areas conditions were substantially aggravated by unknowledgeable methods and poor management in the cultivation and harvesting of agricultural crops.

Russia, in particular, faced serious shortages of staple food products and, to meet this crisis (on a basis that was humanitarian or political, or a combination of both), the federal administration sold huge amounts, particularly of wheat and soya beans, to a needy nation. One can argue about the effects of these transactions upon world peace and upon domestic price levels in the United States. For it was probably true that the siphoning of huge amounts of our crops out of storage converted farm products from a long-term buyers' into a sellers' market.

On the other hand the act went a long way to reverse a policy of subsidies for agriculture that had cost the United States citizens, as taxpayers and consumers, billions of dollars over the years. It changed the policy of withholding acreage from production and again allowed its employment for the growing of crops.

Moreover that was not the entire story. Strange as it may seem, there appears to be a relationship between the recent huge increase in the export of agricultural products and the patently adverse effects of the fuel crisis. As a result of many factors, some of which we have already discussed, the United States has become significantly a have-not nation regarding its possession of fossil fuels. At present, the annual imports of oil into the country total over three billion dollars, and represent half of the nation's 1972 adverse balance of payments in its international trade. The effects upon the value of the dollar in the world's markets have been dramatic and serious; and the future promises a magnification of the problem as it relates to the price of oil, its availability, its effect upon the dollar, and even on the worldwide standing of the United States.

Our stagnant exports, burgeoning imports, and loss of funds have been the adverse results of many influences. But like Horatio at the bridge, one stalwart has stood steadfast and contributed its strength to counter our adverse balance of payments. That has been the large and growing increment in our export of feed. And, in every sense, these cannot be labeled as wasting or eroding assets; for with care and the successful cooperation of man and nature the supply of foodstuffs can be replenished on an annual basis.

So feed and fuel have played this interdependent and interacting role. Feed and food, abetted by the dramatic increase in exports, in consumption, and in their handling costs have risen substantially in price. Fuel promises to follow a somewhat similar course, except that in the case of energy, shortages may be truly critical—because we are dependent first, upon the status of our balance of payments, and second, upon the attitudes and policies of those nations that possess the great proportion of the world's known oil reserves.

So we find that there is a strange but effective companionship between the supply, the demand, and the price of feed and fuel—as disparate as they appear to be. And the length of time this intertwined relationship will endure, depends upon much that is now still unknown.

To a lesser, and less dramatic, degree, the problems of feed production and demand as they apply to milk cows, hogs, and poultry follow the likely course of beef. Little over a half year is necessary for the egg to become a fryer and even a roasting chicken. One and a half years cover the time period of the hog from conception (of 12 live pigs per sow) to the supermarket. Beef, however, has as its own production program, one which requires much longer periods of time to travel the route from womb to butcher. Beef requires a period of nearly a year for gestation and then another two-year period for growing and "finishing" (or fattening). Moreover, the beef animal (like the milk cow) is a relatively inefficient converter of grass, hay, and corn into milk or meat.

To resolve the approaching if not already present crisis in an escalating deficit in supplies of food and their accompanying rise in prices, it is necessary either to reduce demand or to increase the level of supply, or both. It seems almost certain that reduced consumption will come only as a result of changed consumer buying or as a companion of an unwelcome economic recession and a resulting deterioration in the purchase of high-protein foods. And those are ends not to be envied, but rather to be avoided.

The recipe for an increase in the volume of economical beef production requires several ingredients. More land to raise feed will be necessary, plus a cooperative nature to supply sunlight and rain in adequate amounts and at proper times. Unquestionably, it will be essential to use larger amounts of herbicides, insecticides, and chemical fertilizers to increase the soil's fertility and to destroy competition from the power and strength of weeds and insects that reduce the volume and health of the productive crops the farmer seeks to obtain.

New methods of farming must be promoted with even more intensified development and use of sophisticated farm machinery that will plant, cultivate, and harvest more prolific crops per acre from agricultural units of relatively large size. It would be an unhappy but likely result for the trend to continue where the small family farm is absorbed into huge "agrobusiness" complexes, owned by well-to-do domestic and foreign individuals and by syndicates and corporations using public or bank credit and operating multiple farm units distributed by levels of latitudes, so that labor crews and sophisticated machinery can move with the seasons for planting, cultivating, and harvesting. And this would be aggravated if, as in the past, these agrobusinesses benefit not only from large-scale production, but also from the huge government subsidies paid to them, both for raising and *not* raising farm products and crops.

Not only will machinery continue its unbroken trend toward more and more efficient designs and rising costs, but buildings as well, which serve not only as shelters for animals, but also as devices for feeding them with better fodder and with the use of fewer man-hours. These will become, not necessarily more complicated, but more productive. That trend is already visible and progressing reasonably rapidly.

Finally, one can expect great progress in the development

of the animal itself as a means of increasing its effectiveness to produce milk or meat. If increased feed becomes available, the only missing links in the chain of augmenting the supply are the characteristics of the milk cows and beef steer themselves. A more efficient conversion of feed into meat or milk is a much desired goal. Generally, these ends are to be found in the improved genetics of the animals selected, bred, and fed so as to obtain the most efficient production of milk or meat out of the raw material represented by the amount of feed the animals consume.

Usually, the desired results exist in carefully selected high-grade females bred to outstanding bulls (either naturally or by artificial insemination). Under this method the sperm of one prize bull can inseminate hundreds of high-grade cows. However, one female will produce only one calf annually for her ten to twelve useful years for breeding. There is now indicated research development which, hopefully, might make possible the removal of a highly bred embryo from its mother's uterus and its transplantation into the receptive womb of a scrub or pedestrian grade hostess female which will bring her foster son or daughter to full term and give birth to a high-grade offspring. In reality, the calf would not be related to its "incubator mother" which served only to feed, develop, and deliver a get that was neither her sexual doing nor an inheritor of any of her genes.

When, as and if this means of transplanting embryos can be adequately developed, then the upgrading of livestock pretty much around the world will be a matter of decades rather than centuries.

Finally, of course, there remains the very real possibility that protein can be supplied by fish and the mechanical conversion of some types of crops into adequate, even though substitute, equivalents for natural meat.

Fish is an excellent source of protein. But as a supply it is threatened by the inroads being made upon its availability. Increased pollution of the waters has destroyed large segments of the world's fish population. Intensive methods of fishing developed by the Russians, Japanese, Danes, Norwegians, Swedes, and others have overwhelmed the relatively primitive means used by the United States. The waters are being "overgrazed" with the use of modern electronic and manufacturing methodology. And even the areas lying close to the United States coastlines are being overfished by foreign hunters and processors.

The main source of protein as a substitute for meat and fish is the soya bean; other sources would include petroleum, even waste. However, there have already been substantial advances in the conversion of soya beans into products *like* bacon and poultry, among others. The progress made is, as yet, inadequate. Color, texture, odor, and taste apparently have not sufficient appeal to make the substitute food products sufficiently appealing to the average United States housewife and her family. Someday the problems probably will be solved, and the solution may not be too many years distant. However, the relief from our present beef crisis is likely to be sought and *found* in more efficient means of selecting, breeding, and feeding improved herds of cattle.

The needs are great. The avenues of approach are reasonably clear. Our difficulties are qualitative problems; and they will require cooperative effort of science and practical agriculture contributed both by the governmental and private segments.

Hunger lies at the end of a road that leads to failure. Nutrition and better health and physiques will be the rewards of a successful search.

13.
Problems, Problems: Our Imbalance of Payments

As in the past and present, our economy in the future will possess both many problems and much promise. The difficulties are real; the prospects, although uncertain, could be salubrious.

For many generations, the United States took for granted that in international commerce it would always maintain a favorable balance of trade. That meant the foreign demand for our goods and services would exceed what we purchased from abroad. Moreover, throughout the nineteenth century, the United States, as an industrially developing country, could and did depend on older, richer and more established European countries to supply the capital needed in order to build the industry and commerce of a young, but burgeoning, nation. To pay for these loans, imports of machinery, and many luxuries, the United States developed a surplus in exports of raw materials and foodstuffs. As a debtor nation, it was necessary for us to make payments in exports for the interest and principal on the capital loaned. This was done with goods.

However, with the First World War a dramatic shift took place that was augmented by the second global conflict. To finance, in part, the costs of war, our foreign allies sold us large segments of their equities. The United States became a creditor nation.

Generally, economies which have credit balance in their international trade, develop import surpluses, whereas the debtor nations must develop export surpluses. These are necessary in order to pay their debts to foreign lenders.

However, for decades after the United States had become a creditor nation, it did not experience import surpluses. We did not replace a favorable with an unfavorable balance of international trade.

The reasons were many. The United States exported funds in large amounts to debtor nations with which to rebuild old and build new industrial complexes. U.S. travelers went abroad in increasing tidal waves and left billions of dollars all over the globe. Gifts as foreign aid were made in billions of annual increments—representing more than $140 billion in accumulated totals. Uninterrupted payments to the foreign hosts of our hundreds of military establishments furnished for them equivalents of their exports and allowed them to purchase services and goods from the United States and, in turn, gave us the basis of a continued favorable trade balance—even though we had become a creditor nation. Investments by our corporations in foreign branches located within the boundaries of friend and foe alike gave them vouchers, as annual "gift certificates," that were cashed, at least in part, for purchases of U.S. goods.

As a result, in international trade we have had the best of all worlds. We were a creditor nation and, at the same time, we maintained, in international markets, a favorable balance of trade in goods and services.

However, the clouds that were gathering on our economic horizons grew from whisps to thunderheads and then to economic tornadoes. The funds and expertise which, for long spans of time, we had exported abroad helped to convert our world competitors from "journeymen technicians" into highly sophisticated and automated mass producers. Their bases of wages and hourly labor costs were far lower than the high wage levels of the affluent United States. And, so, when relatively inefficient means of production were replaced by highly sophisticated production complexes, the differentials between foreign and U.S. costs as factors in international competition began to make themselves felt. From the contribution made to technology through license agreements and expertise supplied by the United States, there has developed an astonishing improvement in the design, workmanship, and packaging of European and Asian goods. Beauty and quality have been added to the cost advantages of foreign goods and have made them outstandingly successful in the U.S. domestic markets.

It is not difficult to find dramatic and significant samples of preferential purchases of imported goods by U.S. buyers. Low-priced automobiles, radios, television, and microwave ovens represent only a small fraction of the catalog of products successfully offered to and readily accepted in our consumer channels of trade.

Moreover, our dependence upon foreign supplies of fuel and materials was rapidly aggravated. With the impact of increasing demands upon decreasing and restricted domestic supplies resulting from attrition and the successful attacks by well-meaning ecologists and conservationists, the status of availability of our metals and particularly the reserves of fuel for our energy needs changed from national sufficiency to dangerous inadequacies. Therefore, to the increasing problems created by the pressures on our import surpluses, we added the aggravation of necessary purchases from abroad of oil and gas measured in billions of dollars.

Each year, we continued to export more and more of our population as tourists to spend more billions abroad. We maintained our policy of policing and protecting the free world, receiving little if any thanks, but expending dollars in fantastic amounts.

We have exported hundred of billions of dollars in the form of aid, but also as investments in the foreign branches of our domestic multinational corporations.

Within the enrollment of the vast school of second-guessing, there are many who unquestionably will claim that it was easy to see what the problems of the balance of payment *would* be. The quality of "faultless" foresight is not granted to most of us. We can recognize what has happened only after the fact.

Certainly, a series of events, generally not anticipated, developed to bedevil the presumably well-laid plans of men. Several of the nations which had won substantial credit balances in their world-trade operations were unwilling to recognize or accept the usual and to-be-expected results of the overvaluation in international markets of their own currencies and the necessity of a revaluation of the U.S. dollar. Therefore, some created a two-tier system: one for exchange rates in intranational transactions; a second for international trade. For the first, their domestic rates were allowed to float up in relation to the U.S. dollar which continued to retreat. For the second, their rates of currencies in world markets were maintained so that their exports were partially or wholly immune to the usual consequences of a cheaper dollar and a relatively higher price for their domestic currencies.

In addition to pegged or separately classified exchange

rates, some of the creditor countries elected to adopt devices to restrict imports and to maintain their huge export sur-pluses while they were expanding rapidly their positions as creditor nations. The means were various, but chief among them was a series of subsidies to exporting manufacturers, so that their products did not experience the full impact of revaluation (rising prices for their own currencies, declining for the U.S. dollar). In one instance, the devaluation of the dollar in terms of a foreign currency amounted to about 10 percent; and the upward float of their own currencies equaled about the same figure—10 percent. However, the prices of the exported goods of this nation in relation to the dollar rose only 5 percent. Obviously, the mechanism of a free market was not operative. Perhaps that event should have been anticipated. Perhaps it was by some, but surely not by most of us.

To the ailing condition of the U.S. balance of payments, additional bacteria delivered their potent cargoes. Political as well as monetary factors exerted their power. There has developed an almost worldwide intensification of the power of "full employment" as a political goal—and even require-ment. Countries in which employment is importantly related to the level of exports have strong political reasons for protecting exports and limiting imports which, in a very real sense, means the exportation to foreign economies of some of their domestic jobs.

Moreover, both the economic power and currency of the United States is so powerful and so ubiquitous that it is said, "When this nation sneezes, other nations catch pneumonia." The dollar is at present the main world currency, particularly since the true demise or, at least, the recognition of the already existing death of gold as a means of redressing the imbalance of payments in world trade. Finally, the growth of multinational corporations and the huge fund of Eurodollars as a medium of exchange have combined to develop both the U.S. and Eurodollar as a practical currency of business. In addition, hedging operations to protect both their profits and obligations could exaggerate the fluctuations of the dollar. The serious tremors that periodically shake confidence or safety, expand and aggravate, upon a pantographic principle, the resulting effects in the world's money markets.

These sequences are further magnified by the speculators whose interest is not in any economy, but in what profit they can make by buying one currency and dumping another. When in the '20s the so-called Shebas of Germany sold the deutsche mark "short," in carload amounts, they made fortunes for themselves, but they also contributed disaster to a nation and catastrophe to its citizens—and perhaps even a springboard for the later rise of Hitler and his tragic visitations upon mankind.

Periodic devaluations of the dollar represent probably necessary medication to our ailing balance-of-payment problems, but they do not attack the root causes of the difficulties. These, as I have already pointed out, relate primarily to our excessive imports of goods and our exports of payments for services, gifts, military establishments abroad, and capital investments.

The confluence of all these streams of dollars flowing abroad became a raging torrent which has given many nations calls on the U.S. economy and created increasing pressures on the dollar in the world's money markets. The adverse results of these factors might well have been restrained if the surplus of our exports of goods and services had been maintained.

However, the United States continued and even increased the importation of goods and services. Our exports remained relatively stationary while the flood of imports covered our consumer markets to an increasing depth.

The U.S. dollar, because of the relatively high prices of our goods and exports of our funds, became increasingly overvalued. Then we separated the dollar in fact from its theoretical and anachronistic anchorage to a base of gold. We replaced the fixed rate of our currency in the world's money markets with a *floating* rate of exchange. By this qualitative act, we intended to allow the dollar, in its exchange relations with other nations' currencies, to seek its own levels of price. After all, this same economic phenomenon of fluctuating levels takes place in the prices of practically all goods and services.

It was expected that a decline in the value of the dollar as compared to the mark and the yen would presumably make Germany and Japan relatively high- and the U.S. low-priced sources for the purchases of goods and services.

Some progress was made. But our consumers continued to buy more and more imports even with their *depreciated* dollars. The consequence became clear. Obviously, if the quantity of purchases from foreign sources experience not diminution, but expansion, then the very fact of devalued U.S. currency would, of necessity, aggravate the unfavorable balance of both trade and payments. An equal or greater quantity of goods purchased with an increasingly unfavorable rate of exchange must, of course, result in the need for more and more dollars to effect the same quantities of purchases of goods or payments for services.

Even though the rates of rising prices or inflation within our domestic boundaries have increased at about one-half the rate of most other nations, our starting points were sufficiently higher than those of the other economies to ensure the fact that our offerings would compete under price disadvantages.

Unhappily, our unfavorable trade balance has been substantially aggravated by other factors. Our energy crisis has intensified the problems of our adverse balance of payments in international trade. Growing demands combined with a static and even shrinking supply of fuels have made necessary the rapid increase of imports by a nation which for generations had been domestically self-sufficient. Undoubtedly, four wars and the questionable public policies of the pricing of interstate shipments of natural gas, the stricter standards of quality for fossil fuels, and restrictive acts taken against the construction of pipelines and nuclear plants have combined to limit the expansion of the supply of fossil fuels and other forms of energy.

The gates holding back imports have opened wider and wider as increased quotas have allowed, enormously, the importation of oil and gas. And the trend promises to accelerate and expand the many billions of dollars for payment to foreign suppliers into astronomical figures.

The answer to our problems of balances of payment, if there be any, must lie in radical improvement of our competitive position in the markets of world trade, in the expansion of exports, and in the substantial progress, if not solution, of our energy difficulties.

Our problems are indeed serious. But inasmuch as we have created many of them by our sins both of omission and commission, we should be able to see the light and correct most of the errors of our ways.

The proper economic road ahead seems to demand growth: growth in our skills, in our competitive abilities, and in the reserves and production of supplies of energy.

If we should fail to develop the necessary resolutions of our critically adverse balance-of-payment problems through constructive domestic means, then there might well develop another drastically different approach to our difficulties. If we adopt as hypotheses, first, the continuation of the U.S. domestic economy as a relatively superior complex and, second, the maintenance of our unfavorable balance of payments in world trade, then the consequences could well be dramatic, perhaps unpleasant, but probably not lethal.

Under the premises we have set forth, those nations which had developed and were continuing large and favorable trade balances with the U.S. would accumulate increasing amounts of the very limited world supply of gold and huge holdings of U.S. dollars. Their choices would be either in resting on an uneasy mattress stuffed with paper greenbacks of unstable value, or in transferring their surpluses of U.S. currency into significant and expanding investments in our country's domestic industrial and commercial complexes. Then the ability of the markets of the United States to absorb imports would increase in viability and offer sales opportunities to exporters uninhibited by the restriction of local regulations and laws. Moreover, the investments might well prove to represent profitable employment of the creditor nations' excess funds.

This was one of the important aspects of the U.S. economy of the nineteenth century, when it was financed significantly by European capital. It would be a reversal of the trends of the twentieth century, when the U.S. helped greatly to finance the accelerated industrial mechanisms of others. The generation of the twenty-first century might well witness a repetition of the 1800s in the wave of foreign capital exported to the United States. This assumes, of course, that the restrictive measures increasingly applied by other countries—like Canada, France, Japan, Australia, etc.—would not be adopted by the United States in place of its policy of relatively free markets in a relatively free world.

The causes of the critical situation which has developed in our balance of payments are many; but they have their major geneses not in the mechanics of monetary economics, but in the actions of people. And the problem will be either aggravated or ameliorated by the acts of men, not computers.

14.
Crusaders on the March

It is well that the nation is awakening to some of the important problems of its own making. Environmental pollution and exhaustion of the country's natural resources and even of much of the unspoiled landscape, are unhappy harbingers of the future—unless corrective measures are put into effect and kept in force.

It would be sad indeed if the intense interest in this crusade burned itself out or was obscured by a new rallying cry. It would be equally unfortunate if only a few were made the targets, leaving others who are equally guilty unchallenged and uninhibited.

The problems that plague us have been a generation or more in the making, and those who are protesting are to be applauded. But it is unfortunate that many, both in and out of Congress, who are now so articulate and vehement, should have been unaware or silent for so long.

We of the United States apparently have an irrepressible urge to engage in crusades. Some fight for the destruction of the present system without any apparent idea whatsoever as to the kind of society that should or would replace it. They oppose segregation without being certain that the segregated really want integration. Teachers and students alike seek to reform or revolutionize the institutions of higher learning, but they rarely present a blueprint of an alternate plan, or even a reasoned formulation of what they have in mind.

Crusades have much to be said for them, even when they seem to have only a starting point and no settled destination—when the crusaders measure an evil to be attacked, but fail to calibrate all the repercussions of the correctives that may be adopted. The crusaders for environmental protection and ecological balance, wise goals indeed, should take care, however, lest their shots puncture some innocent bystanders. One of their major targets is economic growth. It has been tried in the media and found guilty of contributing to the destruction of man's environment.

Their train of thought may be somewhat tortured but their case is something like this: a practically uncontrolled increase in the quantity of population, instead of a better quality of environment and less pollution for fewer people, has created the constantly growing demand for food, goods, and services. The power and heat demanded have instigated the rape of the land for coal, iron, and oil. And when land resources have run low, the oceans have been exposed to the searching drills, and to the risks of oil leaks and slicks, endangering beaches, waterfront, fowl, and seafood. The use of oil and coal and nuclear power has polluted the air and the water, and damaged, if not destroyed, broad areas of natural beauty.

The mess, they say, has been aggravated by world wars and by the fact that man's skill has outstripped his foresight. He has designed and built millions of automotive vehicles that burn irreplaceable oil and dash about on roads that chew up the countryside wearing out automotive equipment. Cars, trucks, and buses spew noxious monoxide and unburned carbon into the air, and blot out the sun and contaminate the atmosphere. The automobile makers consume millions of tons of steel, glass, paint, rubber, and clean water, and return the water adulterated by the manufacturing process. Their furnaces discharge smoke, gases, oil, and coal into the air.

But there is another side to the story. Assembly-line production of household appliances and automobiles has brought not only more air pollution, but millions of jobs, and has enabled the average family to enjoy comforts and conveniences that their grandparents could not have dreamed of.

The values appear to be worth safeguarding. The problems must be resolved and proper solutions found and kept in effect. However, we must avoid a cure that will benefit the environment but destroy other elements of social well-being. The same bilateral approach should be taken to each of our myriad problems. We should do our utmost to retain the benefits and ameliorate the harmful aspects. And our judgments should be made fairly, objectively, and unemotionally.

The problem of waste products that results directly or indirectly from the activities of human beings, can be solved only by human beings, collectively or individually, whether the individual is the final voice of a large complex of industry, commerce, or government, or of a family. Government can establish laws and regulations to control industry and, incidentally, itself, and it can create instruments of regulation and supervision. The technology is available, but only billions of dollars, well assigned and efficiently spent, and human cooperation, can put the techniques into practice.

The waste products of people create the problem most difficult to solve. Part of the waste products of human beings must be handled, treated, and disposed of, finally, by public agencies. Part comes from industry. This is particularly true of direct pollution by manufacturing; some of it results from packaging that is difficult to dispose of. But much of it is simply litter that is discarded loosely or callously in the parks, on the streets and sidewalks, and in empty lots. Improved methods and techniques of municipal operations, as well as more civic awareness on the part of the public, and perhaps a well-planned decentralized system of penalties and rewards for cleanliness might help.

However, what is euphemistically called solid waste greatly augments pollution. The average person among the 200 million citizens of the United States annually consumes about 1400 pounds of food. Some of this goes into human energy. Some adds to height and weight (desirable or undesirable). However, most of the 1400 pounds is eliminated as liquid or solid waste, eventually carried off as sewage—either treated or untreated—by the rivers and bays that flank most of our communities.

The volume of livestock waste matter exceeds that of humans. There are approximately 121,000,000 head of beef cattle in the United States, each of which consumes about 12 tons of food annually, or 15 to 20 times as much as a human. The waste products of the animal population of the United States is equivalent to that of a human population of about 2 billion. Most animal manure falls on land that drains into brooks, rivers, lakes, or oceans. Some is used as fertilizer. But any crusade for the correction of pollution should include a method for handling the manure of farm animals.

Among the panaceas advanced for the cure of pollution is arresting or reversing economic growth.

Let us assume for the moment that economic but not population growth is arrested. If the population continues to increase fast enough to double itself every thirty-five years or so, with no increase in the sum total of products and services, the amount available per capita will inevitably decrease and the standard of living will continuously shrink.

But if the satisfaction of social and welfare demands are maintained or increased, a stultified growth for the entire economy would mean much higher taxes along with declining standards of living, particularly for the producers in the society.

There may be a basic flaw in the assumption of a correlation between growth and pollution. Many of our large municipalities have grown little, if at all, in the past decade or more. This is true of New York City, in regard to both population and business activity. Nevertheless the pollution in New York—the garbage, dirt, infestation, the befoulment of the air, rivers, and seashore—has increased. Only the chief targets of the antipollutionists—the industries and utilities— have acted aggressively to reduce the level of pollution.

World War II was followed by an unparalleled growth trend, in both production and population, that had positive results, yet exacerbated the environmental imbalance. Perhaps man's progress is bound to create difficulties from which he does not know how to extricate himself. But to advocate poverty and retrogression as antidotes is to adopt a philosophy of despair.

The United States has been plundered of more of its raw materials than any other nation. Two world wars and two undeclared wars have exhausted much of our domestic supply of iron ore, bauxite, copper, and oil. The postwar aid to the Free World and to our former enemies, and the accelerated growth trends within the United States itself, increased the tempo of resource use. Economically, the United States profited from the world wars in the expansion of its productive power and of its world influence, but those benefits were counterbalanced by the acceleration of the rate at which our resources and arable land were diminished, the air and water polluted, and the environment threatened.

15.
The State of Welfare vs.
The Welfare State

Most people, if not all, at least in the free world, would agree that the aim and purpose of an economy, and an entire society as well, is the welfare of its people. Nevertheless, there can be a wide gap between the state of welfare so desired and "The Welfare State" as a means of effecting the desired ends.

There exists, today, a basic difference of attitude and opinion between those who sincerely believe that the state's obligation is increasingly to care for its citizens from the womb to the tomb and, on the other hand, those who regard with increasing distrust and lack of confidence the steady encroachment by public authorities and bureaus upon the initiative, rules, and behavior of the citizens. Then, too, there are those who give fervent obeisance to the belief in economic collectivism that holds that the basic obligation of the individual is to serve the state rather than be served by it.

Speaking for myself, I believe that the primary, if not the sole reason for a political unit is to serve the people, that men and women should work to live rather than live to work, and that the state of welfare of the citizens should be the goal basically of all public agencies.

Even if one accepts this theorem as a whole, there still remain the premises, reasoning, and conclusions which point to the *most* valid and salutory means of effecting the desired purposes.

The welfare state, both in theory and practice, is a rapidly growing mechanism. Its form and substance have been spreading over a substantial portion of the earth's area. And its edicts are often the only ones which its advocates are willing to accept as the proper rules for conduct and correct devices for social progress.

On the other hand, there are others who believe just as sincerely and vehemently that the welfare state is counterproductive to man's proper program of welfare. This school of thought holds that the spreading tentacles of many public activities are strangling individual initiative and stultifying the true bases of progress under the pressure and power of overstuffed bureaus that promote their own functions and expand their own growth. This latter school of thought can often approach a truly Puritan ethic or one in which the plea is frankly made for too little rather than too much government.

Finally, of course, there are some of us who hope that the pendulum will avoid both extremes of its arc and come to rest at its true center point.

We are told that we have a socially bankrupt economy with welfare for the rich and starvation for the poor, and that there must be a radical redistribution of wealth. Apparently, we must use the suction power of government to draw from the well-to-do and pump to the less favored.

This drift toward the welfare state is not new. It has been

rolling along for decades. It got its first and greatest impetus during the early 1930s, and it is practically certain to continue, no matter who is in power. Present developments are unique only in the speed and the extent of change. One can climb north on the slopes of a mountain, going up and up, reach the top and, without changing direction one degree, find that he is going down and down. We are at present spending nearly 40 percent of our gross national product in the public segments, and all of this must come from the millions who are our taxpayers. Many of the various proposals of all political groups are shrouded in the hazy mists of uncertainty and vagueness. However, the core seems reasonably clear and definitive. The plans for increasing governmental expenditures financed by taxes and/or deficits would add to our present public annual expenditures of $400 billion. If this should occur, the expenditures for the public segment could amount to nearly 50 percent of the present gross national product—something less if the economy grew, more if it should shrink.

The welfare state promises, by governmental paternalism, to reduce the power and greed of the "privileged" segments of society and increase the benefits flowing to the mass of the citizens.

We have built a mechanism that spends over 40 percent of our gross national product, and we have employed (beyond the military complement) over 10 million men and women as members of the forces working for governmental projects. And, finally, we have created a fabulous, confusing, and overlapping series of bureaus. They and their drawerlike compartments play essential, albeit confusing roles in the daily living patterns of our corporate units, family groups, and every individual's acts and privileges.

To manage and direct the huge complex that the new,

complete, welfare state will spawn, the bureaucrats will need more power and authority. As Hayek said in *The Road to Serfdom,* collectivism, or socialism or the welfare state, demands first the power of an oligarchy, and later the power of a dictator. Leaders of a Socialist or Communist society may start out with an ideal of beneficent treatment of the common man. But history indicates that they soon convert the benign social organism into a malignancy that metastasizes and spreads its poison through the entire body politic. The more "liberal" the pretense, the more autocratic are the pretenders—whether they are recruited from the economically underprivileged, the politically overprivileged, or even a few among the dwellers in the ivory towers.

The threads and patterns of society's economic and political crazy quilt are strange in their tangles and confusions. The combinations are so numerous and so ramified that an attempt to trace the tangled skeins and the strange designs may prove to be bewildering to reader and author alike.

The welfare state has been born out of the mating of social betterment and political power. In balance, the purpose was probably well intended. The fulfillment is open to many doubts.

Railroads have steadily deteriorated under decades of supervision by the Interstate Commerce Commission (ICC) and the huge subsidies of billions of dollars granted for constructing a crosshatching of the U.S. countryside with strips of concrete highways and superhighways.

Housing for the masses has been promoted by huge grants and favorable tax legislation; nevertheless the press constantly reports messes in those same public housing programs for the masses.

Under well-intended plans to advance a program of promoting welfare, the government of the nation has developed a confused mass of hundreds of bureaus. These are manned by millions of employees, doing good work and unhappily contributing a good deal of confusion, waste, and counterproductive results.

The farm program with its billions of dollars in subsidies contributed out of taxes has added to the burdens of the taxpayers and has significantly increased costs for consumers. The small family farm has withered on the vine; and agrobusiness has grown apace under the dual force of large-scale, highly mechanized production, and significantly larger subsidies—paid alike to local and foreign owners of giant agrobusiness units. Lower costs, derived from expert, efficient mass-production methods, have been combined with high and increasing profits—and, as a consequence, the capital and incentive to expand further the volume of earnings for the owners and of nutrients for the undernourished planet.

Add to this extraordinary potpourri of contradictory and counterproductive themes the advocacy of little or no future growth in production and services, and the inevitable result is a shrinking standard of living. If supply remains static and population continues to grow at a geometric rate, there will be less and less of everything for more and more appetites and needs and desires.

The areas and power of the welfare state are huge and continuously expanding. Whether, in the long run, man will benefit from the aggressive effort to protect him as the ward of the government is open to serious question. But the solution of this conundrum must be contributed either by wise men, self-seeking public officials, or groups of citizens with special interests and privileges.

The movement of the state is toward complete collectivism. As the "protection" of the average citizen "in his best interest" inches forward, so does the need for a powerful oligarchy or bureaucracy to direct and control every citizen for "the good of all." And finally, the large number of governmental bureaus that will have their orbits in the atmosphere of our planet cannot be allowed the freedom to compete and collide with one another. So, in order to control the diverse bureaucracies required, a politburo will develop, and over this group organization there is likely to arise the final and single arbiter—the master of order, the total dictator.

So long as the United States operates, in fact or fiction, under a democratic form of government, it is likely that the members of the oligarchy, the politburo, and the holder of the top post will be "elected" by those in the electorate who are well organized and thus have enough voting power to enforce their will in return for votes.

Will the carefully designed welfare road map lead to the Promised Land? Or again will the best laid plans of men gang agley? Will men grow in happiness and capacity and fulfillment? Or will they lose their sense of self-reliance, independence, and freedom?

Well-intentioned efforts to protect the average individual— usually the consumer—sometimes backfire. Attempts to improve safety of products are proper and desirable. But care must be taken to insure that changes result in more than increases in costs and prices. Too often the regulations and agencies for consumer protection strangle or injure, rather than aid, the competition of free markets to give to the consumers good service and good products. Minimum-wage laws are desirable to prevent unsocially low payments to labor. However, relatively high minima can shift employment away from the young and unskilled to the more expert workers. Wages must be measured not in absolute but relative terms. Only when a higher wage is accompanied by greater productivity will it be conducive to lower costs and competitive advantage. The social aim of minimum wages is admirable. But the schedules may prove counterproductive for the very individuals that the welfare legislation seeks to protect.

A state of welfare for the citizens should be the overriding intent of every society and economy. Whether a welfare state is the best instrument for this purpose is highly debatable.

The advocates of philosophies that hold that the basic requirement of the people is to serve the state are proponents—consciously or unconsciously—of a totalitarian government. Those who hold that the state exists primarily for the benefit of the men, women, and children who make it, eschew the spreading power of the governing instruments and hold that a nation is best governed which is least governed. Such a philosophy is a necessary concomitant of true economic and political democracy.

However, as in many conflicts between the state and the unhampered individual, compromise is essential. Certainly the state has many obligations to the people which only it can fulfill adequately. Defense, police, public works and a hundred other social necessities can be supplied only by the collective grouping of individuals in some form of governmental agency and actions. The state must provide protection of the aged, the ill, and the disadvantaged. However, whether the aid to the needy and the rights of those who provide it can best be served by a welfare state is debatable not only theoretically but also as measured by the record.

The extent to which welfare should be limited is one point at issue. Certainly the needs of those who, with earnest endeavor, cannot provide for themselves should be serviced by those who can. But whether the span should run from the womb to the tomb is subject not only to philosophical and social question but also to grave doubts as to its economic feasibility.

How far a nation can and should go in transferring from

those according to their abilities to those according to their needs must be weighed in the balance of what will supply the greatest good for the greatest number. How heavy a burden can be placed upon those who produce if they must carry the load of those who only consume?

If the productive fail to supply the goods, services, and funds necessary to satisfy the demands of "welfare," then it will be but a matter of time before the national standards for all groups will be eroded, and only poverty will be available for distribution to all.

16.
A Summary
and Some Conclusions

Two threads run through the patterns of practically all the economic fabrics woven by economists in business, labor, trade organizations, banking, academic halls, and government.

The first is a belief that whereas a little inflation may not be too bad a thing, rapid and radical inflation is dangerous— destroying confidence and buying power and security. On how to deal with inflation, however, there is no unanimity. The high priests of the quantitative cult preach fiscal or monetary means, but these seem to have lost some of their potency, if they ever had any. Quantitative measures will *not* control inflation. Prices, except for scarce goods, depend upon the race between factors of costs and efficiency in production and this concept must be expanded to embrace the service segments, now the major part of the U.S. economy.

The second tenet, held by nearly all economists, is that constant *economic growth* is essential. There are few serious and knowledgeable advocates of the principle of economic stability or retrogression.

There is also a general sentiment favoring social betterment. Whether the demands are for better housing, better water and air, better nourishment, better clothing, better education, better medical services, or better opportunity for learning a trade—the unbroken thread that runs through it all is that more funds should be provided by the public segment of our society. But where will the funds come from? How will they be produced? How will payment for the increasing needs be made and by whom?

Under our present system, most of the money for public and social needs comes from taxes on individuals and corporate units. A destruction or paralysis of the growth of the private segment would result in the diminution of earnings and of taxes. Even if taxation is markedly increased, the long-term effect of no growth will be to decrease incentives, contract employment, and reduce volume and profits. The taxes collected would then probably diminish and leave an ever-widening gap between income and outgo.

There are two alternatives. One, is a decrease in the public, social, and civic services that are provided. The second, is a series of constantly increasing governmental deficits, undermining faith in the prudence of the nation and the value of its currency, a prologue to a new version of *The Decline and Fall of the Roman Empire.*

Those who believe most ardently in the expansion of social services should seek most actively to discover the true reason for economic growth and for methods of safeguarding it.

Although many students and experts believe that progressive growth is necessary, they are inclined to stop at that point. They are not agreed on what factors assure growth or what means best guarantee continued economic expansion at the proper rate.

One widely accepted theory is advanced by the school of which Professor Milton Friedman of the University of Chicago is the guru. It holds that the quantity of money that flows into the economy will determine its stability, its progress, its overstimulation, and inflation or recession. But there is flexibility in how "money" is defined, and considerable question and debate as to the inclusion of the velocity of the flow of "currency" by Dr. Friedman's disciples. In any measurement of the effective money supply, velocity is an extremely important factor and is actually a consequence of economic activity. Nevertheless, the monetary school or cult comprises a most impressive blue book of members drawn from banks, corporations, governmental institutions, and academia.

The second heavily traveled route to the land of economic milk and honey is older as an established theory. Its precepts are those of Lord John Maynard Keynes (a noted British economist who had great influence on President Franklin Roosevelt's actions, if not his thinking). Keynesianism is no longer a monolith; large cracks are visible in its solidity, but it is still the economic rock of ages for many. It holds that capital expenditures and public expenditures are the chief means of controlling the economy; and it recommends the use of fiscal devices, like taxes and budget deficits and surpluses, as parts of the mechanism that should be used to keep the economy in a state of equilibrium.[1]

Both the Keynes and the Friedman theories make it seem

---

1. A capsule—and therefore oversimplified—summary of Keynes's theory might include the following: The rate of interest is based on supply and demand for money; investment is determined by rate of interest and profit expectations; level of income and consumption is determined by investment and savings propensity. If the level of income is insufficient to maintain full employment (or so high as to generate inflating tendencies), government tax and spending policies come into force as the equilibrating mechanism.

possible, in fact not too difficult, to control the economy of a nation. The means lie in the manipulation of monetary or fiscal devices. Friedman's theory of the flow of money is the simpler method; but neither approach is complex. Some centralized agency or agencies must make a few important decisions, and if these are put into effect, the economy should be like a smooth sea on which the ship of state can sail serenely from port to port. One could only wish that the state of the economic well-being and of proper price levels could be managed by the turn of a tap that feeds a monetary or fiscal flow into the veins and arteries of commerce, industry, employment, and profits.

But there is another group, an unorganized assemblage of what is less a school than a chorus of wandering minstrel economists. They have no formal ties. Some of them are primitives; many have come up the hard way, observing the pragmatics of economics actually at work in commerce and industry. For a generation I have been a devout member of this small group. If there is any consensus among us, it includes some of the following points:

Currency is important as a mechanism to facilitate trade, and government is an important source of funds for sustaining and stimulating and even overexpanding the national economy. But neither the media of exchange nor the government are the *controlling* economic influences. Prosperity or depression, inflation or deflation—these are determined by the human and sociological factors that control wages and profits and stimulate the purchase of goods and services. If there were no stimuli or incentives to galvanize business, no amount of money or credit or government spending would move the economy from its anchorage. History and logic substantiate this fact. We agnostics wish it were not true; we perversely hope we prove to be wrong, that there is a simple mathematical solution to a complex series of social, scientific, political, and psychological conundrums.

One or more qualitative, not quantitative, stimuli have spurred all our previous periods of growth, and ailing or dying stimuli have brought on all past recessionary trends. When the economy has turned downward, the quantity of production has usually exceeded the demand, and accumulating inventories have forced a production pause. On the other hand, when pessimism reduces levels of production below the levels of consumption, production increases to meet demand and the wheels of industry speed up again.

The emphasis at national and international economic meetings, of governmental debates, of the general run of the house organs of commercial banks and other financial houses is on quantitative factors—chiefly monetary. Keynes, Friedman, and Samuelson differ in detail, but all place their faith in the monetary or fiscal principles of economics.

In spite of my high regard for those men, I think they have been wrong in the past and are failing the future. Public funds make up less than 40 percent of the gross national product and those 400 billion dollars all come from taxes paid by individuals and corporate units or is money borrowed from them.

Nevertheless the funds and acts of government agencies have had a tremendous impact, direct and indirect, and are likely to continue to do so.

Many public expenditures are nationally, socially, and politically essential, but they usually only sustain the economy rather than contribute to its growth. In this category are defense expenditures, welfare costs and unemployment insurance, social security (which is largely self-contained), and funds for government operation. These mainly affect consumption and services, not the production of civilian goods.

Foreign aid and military expenditures abroad are also sustaining economic forces, both to the donor and to the recipients. All of these support the economy, but they will not contribute to growth unless they are *continuously* increased.

Programs like space exploration have different effects. They may improve the image of the United States, but they also advance research and development, particularly in electronics, television, guidance, electronic data control, and new sources of energy. How regenerative they will prove to be, and how high on the list of priorities they belong, is difficult to judge.

In some areas, the partnership of the public and private segments of our economy is absolutely essential. Original experimental ventures may be attempted only if they are financially supported or subsidized by the government. Radically new railroad beds and rolling stock for our deteriorating rail system are cases in point. After prototypes have been designed and built and tested, with the aid of governmental subsidies, the private sector is more than likely to take over and, if allowed to do so, expend ten to a hundred dollars for every dollar granted by the government.

The same is true of the stimulation of U.S. exports. Other countries support their industries' export sales (or tourist travel) by subsidies on prices, special tax benefits, or participation in primary credit risks, or all three. The United States could benefit labor, business, the balance of payments, the nation's economy, and its tax receipts if, instead of exhorting business to increase its exports, it assisted them financially.

Regenerative stimuli usually depend entirely on the partnership of governmental and private segments. Bridges and tunnels that open new areas, flood-control developments, building prototypes of expensive new mechanisms—all must count on government financing. Then the active, aggressive private agencies in our type of economy can convert the small beginnings into broad areas of commercial and industrial development. Modern industry can transform experiments into new enterprises that create growth, add volume, employment, and profits and raise the general standard of living. Cooperation of the public and private sectors has already produced a magnificent series of regenerative projects.

The opinion and policy makers of our nation, particularly those responsible for designing and executing our economic plans, should review, with open minds, the value of their theses to the nation's welfare. They should consider some different, unconventional, opposing points of view. And they should objectively measure the values of regenerative stimuli as contrasted to the flow of money. Finally, our economic pilots should determine the proper course and priorities among the channels and shoals that lie ahead. Too much is involved for any of us to be obstinate about fixed beliefs and prejudices. Our material well-being, even our safety and liberty, may be at risk. The stakes are high.

If the country is to satisfy the proper and increasing demands both of those who produce and those who are not in the position to produce but are nevertheless entitled to consume, and is to satisfy as well the public demands of society itself, then the tempo of growth *must* accelerate continuously. We must remain alert to the importance of maintaining a wise balance between satisfying the needs of the public sector and protecting the equity, incentives, and rewards for those who supply the capital and the production that defray the costs.

Competitive enterprise, with all of its weaknesses and frailties, has proved that it is by far the best system, if social objectives include material well-being. It is essential, however, to analyze the weaknesses of our system and our society, and to discover new and improved means of running our affairs and our lives. But the ferment with no constructive ends will only erode the strength and quality of our society.

The United States lives on what should be a happy triangle—happy if its geometric design is safeguarded. One base angle is a remarkably complex, ingenious, and creative mechanism of production and distribution. The second base angle is the practice and principle of high-dollar wages. The apex encompasses government activity for defense, for subsidies for research and development that are beyond the reach of a single competitive enterprise, and for supplying more and better services for the public well-being and for the poor.

The true character and nature of the United States as a nation and as an economy deserve careful and constant examination, but not vehement, unreasoning, unilateral denigration. We cannot afford to play blindman's buff with the economic fate of our nation.

If controlling the flow of currency and fiscal policies (however defined) will really maintain a prosperous, noninflationary and progressively advancing economy, then we should assure ourselves of adequate statistical equipment and of the best experts to program and interpret the facts. And the sooner the better!

If, on the other hand, the necessary control and the growth of the economy depend upon qualitative, rather than quantitative factors, an adequate and accurate list of projects, in proper priority, should be carefully prepared, researched, and reviewed. To implement this approach to our economic stability and progress, there should be an agency equivalent to the bodies that now determine monetary and fiscal policies. The group dealing with the qualitative elements of the economy should have the expertise and intelligence to set priorities that would create regenerative stimuli. Statesmanship, progressive government, private planning, careful design and development, promotion, and subsidies should set the tempo of economic growth.

Needs, desires, hopes, and aspirations loom, mountain-high, across the threshold of every American home, from the White House to the humblest shack. Growth is necessary to assure progressive social and individual well-being, *but its rate and tempo must be continuously measured,* perhaps restrained, and hopefully, quickened. This thesis is firm and basic, and it is equally valid for a competitive-enterprise economy, a welfare state, or a socialist dictatorship.

* * *